MANAGING
THE
OLDER WORKER

MANAGING THE OLDER WORKER

How to Prepare for the New Organizational Order

PETER CAPPELLI

AND

BILL NOVELLI

HARVARD
BUSINESS
PRESS
Boston
Massachusetts

Library of Congress Cataloging-in-Publication Data

Cappelli, Peter.
  Managing the older worker : how to prepare for the new organizational order/ Peter Cappelli and Bill Novelli.
    p. cm.
  ISBN 978-1-4221-3165-7 (hardcover : alk. paper)
1. Older people—Employment. 2. Age and employment. 3. Personnel management. I. Novelli, William D. II. Title.
  HF5549.5.O44C37 2010
  658.30084'6—dc22

                                                        2010013250

To our families

To Virginia, Michael, and Bo

To Fran Novelli and our (working)
children, and to our wonderful
grandkids, who will be among
the workers of tomorrow

Contents

Foreword

The twentieth century was transformational. It will be remembered as a time when life expectancy almost doubled for developed and developing countries alike. Living to a ripe old age has become the norm. People today expect to live into their eighties and beyond, and as the twenty-first century unfolds, more and more people are planning and living their lives accordingly.

In yesterday's world, most people went through a fairly sequential pattern in their lives: education was for the young, work was for adults, and leisure (retirement) was for the old. But that pattern has changed. Age no longer defines what we do in our lives, or when we do it. Today, more than ever before, there are more twists and turns in the road. This is especially evident in the workplace. Just as the population is getting older as a result of the aging of the boomers and people living longer, so too is the workforce. People are working longer, out of either choice or necessity. Some retire and then go back to work, others start their own businesses, and still others work part-time for pay and volunteer part-time.

This trend is having a disruptive influence in corporate America as businesses struggle to find ways to manage their intergenerational workforces effectively and figure out how to get the most out of their workforce that will include a larger proportion of older workers. This is an issue that we care deeply about at AARP as more and more of our members want or need to keep working past traditional retirement age. We have been working for years to help both older workers and employers bridge the gap, to facilitate the shift to an older workforce. We have created a number of programs and initiatives to achieve this, many of which are referenced in this book.

In *Managing the Older Worker: How to Prepare for the New Organizational Order*, authors Peter Cappelli and Bill Novelli discuss the changes we are experiencing today in adapting to an older workforce. In many ways, these are similar to those I experienced when I began my career as a sales trainee with Xerox in 1968. At that time, the issue was not how to deal with an influx of older workers; it was how to deal with the increasing numbers of women and minorities in the workforce. In both cases, there are significant lessons to be learned about the power of inclusion.

I believed then, as I do now, that inclusion of diverse populations—including older workers—is America's strength. At Xerox, we achieved outstanding results with the most diverse workforce (at all levels) in any of the *Fortune* 500 companies. We became a more inclusive and better company. We demonstrated that diversity is America's strength. And in May 2009, Xerox announced Ursula Burns as the first black female CEO of a *Fortune* 500 company.

Embracing diversity has been a long and continuing journey for corporate America. The struggle today to embrace older workers is a continuation of that journey. The parallels are striking. As Cappelli and Novelli point out, it begins with a commitment from the top. At Xerox, it began in 1968, when Joseph C. Wilson, founder of the modern Xerox, and C. Peter McColough, then president of Xerox, sent a letter to all Xerox managers making them personally responsible for the company's success in increasing diversity. They made the case not only that this was a moral imperative, but that it gave Xerox a business advantage over its competitors. They recognized that as its customer base was becoming more diverse, the company would benefit from a more diverse workforce. The business case for older workers, described in chapter 3, is just as compelling. And in chapter 7, Cappelli and Novelli talk about how changing marketplace demographics are creating an older customer base for many companies.

It's not enough to have strong leadership at the top—corporate cultures must also change in order to get the most out of an older workforce. But changing corporate culture takes time, even with strong leadership from the top. Throughout this book, the authors confront this head-on, dispelling the myths about older workers, confronting ageism, and helping younger supervisors.

The lesson here with regard to older workers is clear. It's one thing to retain and recruit older workers, but it's quite another to make them truly part of the company, where their ideas, experience, and insight are valued throughout the entire organization. I recall at Xerox, David Kearns, who later became chairman and CEO, found that many of the concerns raised by African American, Hispanic, and women employees were also shared by other workers. Often when a manager was judging an employee based on race or gender instead of performance, that manager was probably judging other employees on equally arbitrary standards. It strikes me that today this may also be the case when a manager arbitrarily judges an employee based on age, or their misperceptions about age. This book offers practical suggestions to help identify and change this behavior.

Companies that fail to adapt to societal changes, including increased diversity and aging populations, risk stagnation that comes from being mired in the old way of doing things. That's one of the reasons that nearly 80 percent of the companies that made up the *Fortune* 500 forty years ago have disappeared. As I discovered at Xerox, and later as CEO of Avis Holdings, successful companies today need a creative, motivated workforce of problem solvers who can work collaboratively to anticipate customer needs and envision new markets and who are committed to quality and productivity. Workers with different backgrounds, experiences, and perspectives help create this kind of workplace where innovative solutions can blossom. Experience tells us that companies ruled by a hierarchy of imagination and innovation, and filled with people of all ages, races, and backgrounds, are the most successful.

Most corporate leaders today understand and accept the business advantage of a diverse workforce. But far fewer see older workers as part of that mix. They fail to accept the advantage gained by retaining, retraining, and recruiting older workers. That's why this book is so important for today's corporate leaders and managers. Cappelli and Novelli explain the older worker phenomenon and what it means for employers, managers, and employees alike. They carefully guide readers through the research on older workers (much of it conducted by or commissioned by AARP), lay out the business case for retaining and hiring older workers by highlighting those companies that have proven strategies to address the needs of a multigenerational workforce, and offer concrete suggestions on how to manage and take advantage of an older workforce. They also talk about this as a practical business response to a changing, growing, and more affluent older consumer marketplace, and they raise the public policy issues that must be addressed with regard to older workers.

At AARP, we believe that everyone needs to understand the unique issues and challenges faced by a growing older population that is forward looking, focused on the future, and continuously asking "What's next?"—especially as they relate to the workplace and the marketplace. Only by understanding their diversity of lifestyles, wants, needs, and expectations can we take advantage of all they have to offer and ensure that all people have their shot at the American dream. *Managing the Older Worker: How to Prepare for the New Organizational Order* is corporate America's guide, not just for understanding these issues and challenges, but also for adapting to change and getting the most out of an older workforce.

—Addison Barry Rand, Chief Executive Officer, AARP

Addison Barry Rand spent more than thirty years at Xerox, rising through the ranks from a sales trainee to executive vice president of worldwide operations. He left Xerox to become CEO of Avis Holdings and later served as CEO of Equitant Ltd. He took over as CEO of AARP in April 2009.

Preface

This book is about one of the most important challenges facing all companies today, in the United States and around the developed world. With the growing number of older workers in the workplace or trying to get back in, and as the baby boomer generation "retires retirement" and stays in the workforce longer, it is now becoming more and more common to find older workers being managed by younger managers. This reversal of the traditional reporting hierarchy, seen in more and more organizations, introduces a new set of challenges for younger managers and older workers alike.

Older workers are a tremendous resource for employers, but they are having great difficulty being accepted back into organizations. The main constraint is conflicts and misunderstandings with younger managers. To oversimplify, younger managers don't really know how to manage older workers—and older workers don't know how to get what they need from their younger managers. In the chapters that follow, we describe the opportunities that the rapidly expanding older workforce offers employers; the challenges that at present stand in the way of engaging these workers, particularly with their younger managers; and specific strategies and practices for younger managers to manage more effectively their older workers.

The Growing Dilemma

Individuals in society want to work longer and will need to do so in order to support longer and healthier lives. They don't always want to keep doing the same jobs, they generally want to work less in terms of hours and effort, and they clearly have different priorities about the outcomes they want from work. But a huge majority want to keep working. The difficulty that they face in securing employment relates in part to misunderstandings about their abilities, in part to management practices that don't allow employers to engage them, and in part to outright prejudice. Discrimination against older individuals is common and especially pernicious because it eventually affects everyone, if we have the good fortune to live long enough.

At the same time that we see widespread discrimination against older workers, employers are complaining about not being able to get workers with the skills and competencies they need, especially strong work ethics and good interpersonal skills. These are exactly the competencies that older workers offer. Employers are tying themselves in knots trying to figure out how to engage young workers, fixating on trivial differences in the interests of Generation X, Generation Y, Millennials, and whatever name comes next, while ignoring the massive and permanent workforce represented by older workers. As we argue below, older workers are not necessarily more expensive than their younger colleagues, and they perform better on virtually every relevant aspect of job performance. But the most powerful case for retaining existing older workers and bringing on new ones relies on their ability to meet demands that other workers cannot. These include the following:

- Helping with the problem of knowledge transfer between generations, an issue rooted in the fact that older workers have a lot of tacit knowledge that their younger peers have yet to acquire.
- Solidifying culture. Experienced workers know the norms and values of the organization and are able to pass them along to new hires, especially through formal "partnerships" that pair up older and younger workers.

- Mentoring. Experienced employees, especially those who have finished their careers and are officially retired from their firms, make excellent mentors for younger employees as the former know a lot about the organization, no longer have a personal stake in office politics and can be objective, and typically are at the point in their lives where altruistic goals become more important. They make excellent coaches.
- Most importantly, serving as a "just-in-time" workforce for special projects, meeting peak demands in business, and other one-off needs. Using retired employees saves the organization all the "on boarding" costs of a new hire, or even bringing in a temp or contract worker, and the retirees also know the culture and the operating procedures of the organization. The word on every CEO's lips after the financial meltdown and associated recession is *flexibility*—how we are able to scale down and then scale back up quickly when circumstances change. Older workers provide that flexibility. Older workers provide exactly what employers say they need at the same time that there is widespread discrimination just in keeping them in organizations, let alone bringing them back in.

Who Are the Older Workers?

The challenges and also the opportunity offered by an aging workforce begin with demographics. Most observers think that the aging of the baby boomers is the important factor driving a big expansion of older individuals, and there is no doubt that it matters a lot. But the biggest factor by far is growing life expectancy, something that will continue after baby boomers pass from the scene. The fact that people are living longer and therefore both need and want to keep working is the issue.

When does one become a mature or older worker? Part of the definition relates to chronological age, but the more important component may be one's stage in their working life. We define older workers as those who are experiencing a fundamental change in their employment relationship that is related to age, most often employer driven through retirement policies or layoffs late in one's career that cause individuals to seek new jobs or work in a different way. The most common of the different approaches is to keep working beyond the usual retirement age, but other challenges include working in a different way—something other than full-time, for example, in roles that are usually seen as full-time—or changing direction completely. We traditionally thought that individuals changed careers or went back to school early in their working life. Now that is happening for people who are much older, who have already worked for thirty or forty years. That juxtaposition of an older individual following what had been a younger person's path is creating new challenges.

The most fundamental challenge, though, is simply to get and keep a job when one is older. Most individuals who approach the traditional retirement age of sixty-five want to keep working in some capacity, but most end up not doing so. And the reason has to do with a lack of opportunity. Another way to define when one is an older worker, therefore, is when age-related prejudice kicks in: for some jobs it may be as young as forty, and indeed in the United States that is when legislative protections against age discrimination begin. In professions and other fields where skills are portable, it may be much later, into the sixties.

The Employer Side of the Equation

Why is it that we have such a hard time continuing to find work as we grow older, especially as employers complain about not being able to find workers with the right attitudes, who have the skills to "hit the group running," and who can make immediate contributions? One would think employers would be falling over themselves to retain older employees, to let them keep working in more flexible ways, and to hire other older workers. But they are not.

There may be many reasons why older workers are not able to find opportunities to keep working, but most of them have to do with misperceptions about older workers. These are so widespread yet without basis that they can be thought of as myths, and they include the following: older workers don't perform as well as younger workers, they demand high pay and cost a lot more, they don't want to change, they won't take a step down in role, and so forth. Discrimination against older workers is widespread—indeed, by most measures, greater than that confronting minorities and women.

And the biggest obstacle in getting access to jobs lies with younger managers. The biggest concern about hiring older workers expressed by employers is that conflicts would result when they are managed by invariably younger supervisors. An incredible 88 percent of employers worry about hiring older workers because of such conflicts.

The heart of the difficulty of getting older workers into successful work relationships lies with the challenge of having younger managers supervise employees who are older than they are. Research suggests conclusively that both younger managers and their older subordinates distrust each other and that negative attributions on both sides are common—although frankly much more common among younger supervisors than older subordinates. The cause appears to have less to do with the age differences per se and more to do with the difference in experience and the way in which younger managers try to supervise their more experienced subordinates.

Managing older workers, therefore, requires a different approach. It is not one that is untested, however, and it conforms to many of the contemporary ideas about effective leadership, from the military down to start-up firms: communicate clearly about issues and challenges, involve employees in decisions, delegate tasks, and recognize contributions. Above all, acknowledge what the older subordinates know.

Older Workers in the Movies

The experience of older employees being managed by younger supervisors came to the big screen with the 2004 movie *In Good Company*. In it, Dennis Quaid plays a successful middle-aged salesman who is demoted to make room for a much younger outsider. The plot plays out all the age-related stereotypes: the older man is portrayed as humiliated at having to work for the younger, inexperienced boss, who in turn is presented as being ruthless and having a single-minded ambition. Having the younger executive manage the older and more experienced man is depicted as not only unnatural but dysfunctional. The two battle for control over workplace priorities, and the conflict between them eventually gets resolved when they bond over a last-ditch work project. Their relationship in the end evolves into a traditional father–son model that largely ignores the fact that the younger executive is still the boss.

Management Practices for Older Subordinates

Older workers are a tremendous asset for almost any organization. In terms of work ethic, absenteeism, and turnover, they score better than their younger peers. But they are not identical to their younger colleagues. In particular, their reasons for working are often different and can lead to mismatches with the management practices of many employers. Beyond the interaction with supervisors, older workers benefit from a somewhat different employment model, although it is not so different that it need shake the basic assumptions of the organization.

Many and arguably most large employers motivate employees with money, with promises of promotions and career advancement, and at least implicitly with the fear of being fired if they don't perform. None of these factors matter as much to older individuals, who are near the end of their career. Attracting and then engaging the older workforce begins with a different and distinctive value proposition that includes giving greater importance to a sense of mission; serving a social purpose or at least one that goes beyond simply making money for shareholders; offering flexibility in terms of work schedules; and offering greater choice in benefits that might include some targeted to older individuals (e.g., elder care insurance along with day care programs). An interesting point about the above list is that it is not unlike a list we would see generated to attract young workers. In fact, the interests of older and younger employees are highly similar. Perhaps it is those in the middle who represent the more unusual case.

More generally, employers interested in making better use of the mature workforce should begin with opportunities to extend the working life of their own employees. Some companies expand these opportunities to alumni of their organization, those who may have left before retirement. And a few novel arrangements have developed where companies make their retirees available to each other, effectively swapping them back and forth.

Overall, efforts to make better use of older individuals in the workplace represent one of the greatest opportunities available for improving society. It is about the only way to provide the resources necessary to pay for longer lives; it helps address exactly the needs employers say they have for a skilled, just-in-time workforce; and it provides some of the best opportunities for older individuals to stay active and engaged. The arguments are so compelling that they may seem inevitable. The question is simply how long it will take and whether your organization wants to be at the front of that trend, getting the benefits first, or losing out by trailing behind. This book tells you how to get on board.

Acknowledgments

This book is based on the contributions of hundreds of scholars from many different fields. Although it is impossible to acknowledge all of them, we are especially indebted to Ruth Kanfer at Georgia Tech, Neil Charness at Florida State University, and Sara Czaja at the University of Miami for guidance through the psychological literature on aging. AARP continues to be the most important resource for those interested in older workers, and our colleagues Deborah Russell and Sara Rix there were especially helpful. We also drew extensively on the resources from Boston College's Center for Retirement Research. Lynn Selhat conducted the interviews for the book, organized the initial project, and played a crucial role in preparing the first draft. Boe Workman of AARP was a valuable sounding board and contributed especially to the ideas and structure of the concluding chapter.

PART ONE

Dispelling the Myths
About Older Workers

1

The Older Worker Phenomenon

The era where employees worked full-time until they hit their sixty-fifth birthday has given way to a frenzy of restructuring blitzes and early retirement programs that got rid of workers long before they reached retirement and replaced them with younger recruits. As employers fretted about whether they would be able to please each new age group of workers coming along—Millennials, Gen Y, X, or whatever—they also started to complain about the difficulty in finding skilled and dependable workers.

Into this picture comes Pitney Bowes, the mail systems company headquartered in Stamford, Connecticut. Almost 20 percent of its *new hires* have been over age fifty. It is hanging onto retirees, bringing them back for short-term assignments and staffing a pool of temp employees from its retiree population. The company is piloting a program that allows retirees to take short-term assignments in warmer climates—Florida in the winter, for example—to combine work and traditional retirement.

For current employees, the company has a "My Next Phase" program to help them identify their interests and skills and think about job opportunities for the future, including career changes. Its Retirement Education Assistance Program for employees over age forty-five pays for classes to help with retirement planning that may include how to keep working. In terms of benefits, long-term health care has been added to the list of options, and the employee assistance plan includes assistance with elder care.

To make it easier to engage older workers, the company has embarked on more flexible work schedules, job sharing, and telecommuting. It uses a self-service, ergonomics software tool to identify jobs that might cause injuries and to suggest modifications in work tasks. And it provides on-site health clinics and fitness centers. While these programs are good for all workers, they are of special interest to older employees.

The reason Pitney Bowes and companies like it are moving in this different direction is because it pays for them to do so. Why it makes sense for employers to engage older workers and how to overcome the challenges that keep them from doing so is the subject of this book.

The Expanding Number of Older Workers

The older worker phenomenon begins with the fact that there are now, and will be as far into the future as we can see, one heck of a lot more older workers than ever before. The reason why is a bit different than what many people think.

Baby Boomers

There are three separate parts to the equation that explains the expanding number of older workers. The first one has gotten the most attention but may well be the least important of the three, the baby boom cohort. The basic facts of the baby boom generation are well known: the prosperity that followed WWII led to a sharp increase in the birth rate in the United States. The baby boom cohort, born between 1946 and 1964, stands out in contrast both to a "baby bust" period of low birth rates during the Depression and into WWII and to a period of declining birth rates after 1964. The latter can be traced to more reliable birth control but also to better opportunities for women in the labor market.

The image of a python swallowing a pig—a bulge slowly moving along over time—is often used to illustrate the changes in the distribution of the U.S. population as the large baby boom cohort grows older, first stretching the capacity of the school systems when they were young, then having the same effect on colleges, entry-level jobs, and every other institution that they have touched, and now moving into what we have traditionally thought of as the retirement years. While it may be cool to be part of the boomer cohort because it has the tendency to shape popular culture to its own needs, in terms of tangible outcomes such as access to education, jobs, and housing, it's been a bad deal for those in it because of the competition associated with so many peers and the difficulty that social institutions have had at every step of the way in accommodating the size of this huge cohort.[1]

As baby boomers grow older, the number of people who are "old" will also rise, as will the proportion of the total population that is older. For example, in the period 2000–2010, the number of people in the United States age forty-five to sixty-four, where the baby boom is centered, grew by 18,573,000; the number in the age group ahead of them (sixty-five to eighty-four) grew by only 3,326,000; and the number in the cohort just behind them (age twenty to forty-four) grew by even less, 369,000. In the next decade, 2010–2020, the baby boomers will move into the sixty-five-to-eighty-four age group, swelling it by 13,243,000 (less than the number currently age forty-five to sixty-four because of expected mortality).[2]

The aging of the baby boom will clearly represent a significant expansion of the population of older individuals, but two more factors are even more important to the aging of the population and especially to the labor force.

Longer Life Expectancy

Although the aging of the boomers gets all the popular attention, growing life expectancy is actually a much more important factor in shifting the distribution of the population toward older age groups. Unlike the baby boom, which will eventually pass and be replaced in the ranks of older citizens by the smaller baby bust cohort, extended life expectancy should be a permanent feature for each new generation. Indeed, it should continue to expand into the future, and therefore the population of older workers will forever be bigger because of increasing life expectancy.

The U.S. National Institutes of Health calculates that the life expectancy of a baby boomer born in 1950 was twenty years longer than for an individual born in 1900; those sixty-five years old in the mid-2000s will live about seven years longer than their counterparts who were sixty-five in the 1960s; a baby born in 2010 will live about ten years longer than the boomers born in 1950.[3] Those extra years, and more in the future, by definition come at the end of life. They add more years to what we now think of as the "older" age group, say, those over age sixty-five, shifting the distribution of the population toward the oldest age groups.

The importance of additional life expectancy is not just that people live longer but that they are healthier longer. The improvements in lifestyle and health care that cause people to live longer also help them to avoid the impairments and disabilities of illness and disease (see "Living Longer and Healthier"). The additional years of health and vitality may not be completely identical to the additional years of life expectancy, but they are close. Improved health and life expectancy might cause us to rethink our assumptions about what constitutes "old."

Living Longer and Healthier

A series of new studies examines long-term trends in health in the United States beginning with the medical records of Civil War veterans. Even more important than the improvements in longevity over time have been the gains in health and vitality. The miracles of antibiotics to treat infectious diseases and of surgeries to treat other conditions are well known, but the biggest improvements may be in chronic illnesses. Virtually everyone in the late 1800s was sick most of their lives, primarily from chronic illnesses associated with aging. Eighty percent of the Civil War veterans had heart disease by age sixty, an age-related illness, versus about 50 percent of sixty-year-olds now. And, of course, a great many more died from these illnesses before even hitting age sixty. Other chronic diseases, like arthritis and lung ailments, have not gone away, but they happen ten to twenty-five years later than during the Civil War era. The important explanation for the improvement in chronic disease appears to be improvements in diet and health during pregnancy and then in the infant years: being healthier as a baby seems to be the key. The average American now not only is healthier but, as a marker for that health, is three inches taller and fifty pounds heavier than their Civil War ancestors.

Source: Gina Kolata, "So Big and Healthy Grandpa Wouldn't Even Know You," *New York Times,* July 30, 2006.

Stanford economist John Shoven shows how the picture of the older workforce changes when we define *age* in terms of health and life expectancy rather than years of life. A 1 percent chance of dying in a year is pretty low for adults, and that is what we usually associate with being in the prime of adult life (*prime-age* workers are defined by government statistics as being age twenty-five to fifty-four). He calculates that in 1970, fifty-one years was as old as men could get and still face only about a 1 percent risk of dying; by 2000, they could be as old as fifty-eight—age sixty-three for women. Individuals at the typical retirement age of sixty-five in the 2000s have a risk of dying that is about the same as those in their midfifties in the 1970s. While the number of individuals who are age sixty-five will grow by 66 percent by 2035, the number of individuals who will be sick enough to face the same risk of dying as a typical sixty-five-year-old does today will only increase by *less than 16.5 percent* over the same period, a huge difference.[4] In other words, the population will gain lots more people who are still quite healthy as measured by having a low risk of death. The way to think about all this is that older individuals in terms of age will be a lot younger in terms of their health and life expectancy than ever before.

If we think of *old* as being defined by *how many more years we have to live*, rather than *how many we have lived already*, the picture changes a lot. First, there will be little growth in the population that meets this alternative definition of *old*. To illustrate, if we define *old* as being those who are likely to live less than fifteen more years, people who were roughly sixty-four would have been old in 1950, as indeed we thought of them at the time. But in 2010, only those more than age seventy-one would be considered old by the same definition. Defining *old* in terms of remaining life expectancy means that the percentage of the population that is old should actually start to *decline* over time. The reason is that the additional years of life expectancy are effectively added to the prime-age category, those with more than fifteen years of remaining life expectancy, rather than to the end of life, when infirmities and illness are most common.[5] In that case, we should expect the effects on the labor force to be huge. If men in the future retire with the same years of remaining life expectancy that they have now—in other words, if the years of additional life expectancy are added to their working life—it will expand the size of the entire labor force in 2050 by about 10 percent. If women did the same, the effect would be even bigger. (See figure 1-1.) These would be

FIGURE 1-1

Age of mortality milestones for men and women, 1940–2000

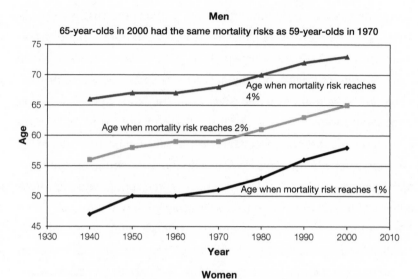

Men

65-year-olds in 2000 had the same mortality risks as 59-year-olds in 1970

Age when mortality risk reaches 4%

Age when mortality risk reaches 2%

Age when mortality risk reaches 1%

Women

63-year-olds in 2000 had the same mortality risks as 59-year-olds in 1970

Age when mortality risk reaches 4%

Age when mortality risk reaches 2%

Age when mortality risk reaches 1%

Source: adapted from John B. Shoven, "New Age Thinking," working paper 13476 (Cambridge, MA: National Bureau of Economic Research, October 2007).

enormous increases in the size of the labor force, increases that would swamp the arrival of the baby boomers and, more importantly, would be permanent.

Decisions to Join or Leave the Workplace

The longer life expectancy leads us directly into the third factor shaping the phenomenon of the older worker, and that is the decision such workers make about whether to seek jobs. That decision determines what economists refer to as the *labor force participation rate*, the percentage of individuals who are either working or seeking a job. Permanent withdrawal from the labor force—no longer working, looking for work, or intending to work—is for older individuals the most common definition of retirement. It is interesting to note that when younger workers do the same thing, we call them *discouraged workers*, those who have given up looking for jobs because it is so difficult to find what they are looking for. But when individuals are older, we assume that this was their choice, and we call it retirement. As we will see later, many of the older workers don't actually choose to stop working; they are in fact discouraged from continuing by a lack of opportunities. Whether these retirement decisions will change based on the availability of jobs is an important issue we consider later.

The choices about working and the labor force participation rates that follow from them differ a lot not only across age groups but also between men and women. Arguably the biggest story in the labor force since WWII was not the baby boom but the rising labor force participation rates of women, who now are much more likely not only to go to work after leaving school but especially to stay in the labor force after they marry and have children. The increase in the percentage of women who are in the labor force coincided roughly with the entry of the baby boomers into the workforce, and the two factors together led to a substantial increase in workers. The growth of the workforce associated with the baby boom has therefore been even bigger than the growth of the baby boom cohort itself because so many more women decided to work. The labor force participation rates of men, in contrast, actually declined somewhat, especially for those age fifty-five to sixty-four. In 1989, only 67 percent of men in that age group were in the labor force, down from 87 percent in 1969. Men age sixty-five to sixty-nine also saw a somewhat more modest decline, from 73 percent participation in 1969 to 64 percent in 1989 (see figure 1-2).[6]

How much of this shift toward retiring at an earlier age was the result of a lack of opportunities to keep working versus having the means and inclination to stop working is something we consider more carefully later in the book. What is most interesting about this development, however, is that the move toward retiring earlier came about at the same time that life expectancy was growing significantly. Both factors were pushing in the same direction to create substantially longer periods of retirement. John Shoven calculates, for example, that about 80 percent of men with fifteen years of life expectancy remaining were in the labor force in 1965. By 2005, that percentage had fallen to only 15 percent.[7] Now we can see why the

FIGURE 1-2

Labor force participation rate of workers 65 and over, 1948–2007

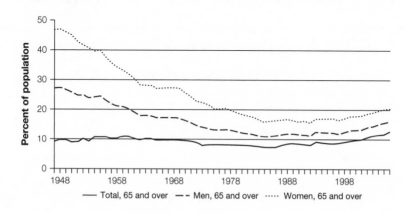

Source: U.S. Bureau of Labor Statistics, http://www.bls.gov.

three factors noted above all have to be taken into consideration when we're thinking about the older workforce: the baby boom means more individuals will be around at age sixty-five or older; increased health and life expectancy means each older individual will be around longer and be more able to do things. These factors become especially powerful if these older, healthier individuals then make the decision to keep working.

From the 1960s on, the trend had been for individuals to stop working at a younger age, at least for men. But now the tide seems to have turned. Since 1985, the labor force participation rate of older men, age sixty-two to seventy, has been rising, and since 2001 it has been rising for both men and women over age sixty-five. More important, the percentage of workers in their fifties who expect to work beyond age sixty-five has risen from the 1990s to the 2000s, an issue we take up later.[8] If the trend toward higher labor force participation rates continues, the older workforce will grow very sharply (see figure 1-3) because all three of the above factors will be pushing in the same direction: more individuals over age sixty-five, more of

FIGURE 1-3

Projected percentage change in labor force by age, 2006–2016

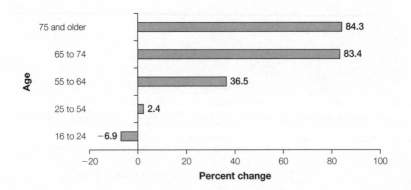

Source: U.S. Bureau of Labor Statistics, http://www.bls.gov.

those are healthy and living longer, and more decide to work and to stay working longer.

When we look back on these three factors shaping the older worker phenomenon, only the decision to work is capable of being influenced by employers and workplace policies. Those policies are the focus of this book.

Why Have Retirement?

If someone from another planet were looking at the phenomenon of older workers, what might be most puzzling is that so many people stop working completely, all at once. And in historical terms, this path is a new development. In previous generations, individuals were much more likely to phase out of work gradually, especially those involved in farming and small businesses. Historian Dora Costa reports that the retirement age of sixty-five got a big boost in 1883 when it became the official age for government pensions in Bismarck's Germany. It was then picked up by the U.S. government as the age at which Union army veterans could receive a pension. (Life expectancy in both countries was well below age sixty-five, which made the pensions a pretty cheap deal for the governments.) Before then, men had to keep working in order to have the income to live. She reports that the labor force participation rate of men over age sixty-four in the United States fell from 78 percent in 1880 to 58 percent in 1930, in part because of pensions. By 1934, age sixty-five became the official retirement age in the United States when the Social Security program was created. Retirement then accelerated, so that by 1990, only 30 percent of men over age sixty-four were in the labor force.[9]

Not only were individuals withdrawing from the workforce at age sixty-five, they now did so abruptly. In the period from 1969 to 1979, for example, 75 percent of men who retired went directly from full-time work to full-time retirement.[10] That was the model, full on to full stop. A generation after 1979, retirement has changed, but not as much as one might expect. If we look at individuals age fifty-one to seventy-one, 58 percent left work altogether, and we describe that situation as being retirement. Of those who left, we know that two-thirds said that their health was good, so they were not forced out of work by health problems.[11] Yet when asked what they intended to do, only 25 percent of those age fifty-one to seventy-one who were approaching retirement said that they wanted to stop paid employment altogether. But most of the 75 percent who wanted to keep working ended up not doing so.

A Modern Perspective

It makes perfect sense to want to transition from full-time work to complete retirement gradually as a way of adjusting to changes in life that also happen gradually. With so many of our social connections taking place at work, leaving them completely can be difficult. A more gradual transition to the lower income levels associated with not working also makes for an easier financial transition. Results from surveys of older workers report that what they indeed want to do is withdraw gradually from work, specifically by cutting back on their hours before leaving the labor force altogether. Were they able to do so? Following up with these respondents revealed that only 35 percent of those who wanted to withdraw gradually were actually able to do so. In contrast, two-thirds of those who said they wanted to stop working altogether did, and 85 percent of those who said that they wanted to keep working as they had been, full-time, were able to.

Of those respondents who said that their employer prohibited them from continuing to work with reduced hours, 43 percent stopped working altogether. But only 22 percent of those who said their employer allowed them to keep working with reduced hours gave up work completely. So employer practices matter a lot. Those who were hoping to change the type of work they did were the least successful in achieving their plans.[12] More generally, nearly a third of retired workers report that their retirement decision was not voluntary, that they would like to have remained in the labor force in some way but did not have the opportunity.[13] In other words, the move from full-time work immediately to retirement doesn't seem to be driven by employee choices. Employer practices affect these decisions a lot.

Similar conclusions apply to those who have already retired. A different survey found that two-thirds of older workers were expecting to have some paid employment when they moved into the retirement age, but ten years later, only about half that group had done *any* work for pay.[14] This set of results helps explain the finding from another study that those older workers who were interested in reducing their hours of work were also more likely in a later period to withdraw from the labor force altogether, presumably because the only real option they had for reducing hours of work was to give up and stop working completely because part-time working arrangements were not available.[15]

The difficulty in withdrawing gradually from paid employment at the end of one's working life may also explain why so many older workers become self-employed. Thirty-four percent of all self-employed became so after age fifty. The self-employed have the ability to control their own hours of work much better than those who are regular employees. Compared to regular employees, those who are self-employed are more likely to expect to be working at age sixty-five and are also much more likely to want to reduce their hours as they grow older.[16] Self-employment presents its own challenges and difficulties, but the constraints on being able to work as an older employee make it especially attractive for older individuals.

A Coming Labor Shortage?

Some pundits assert that a labor shortage is coming that will be so severe that employers will have to scramble to find any employees. They will be desperate to hire older workers—or anyone else for that matter—and the discrimination we observe in the workplace will simply evaporate.

There is no evidence to support this view. The facts about what we know are simple. The only credible forecasts of the future labor force are those produced by the government's Bureau of Labor Statistics (BLS). They suggest that the U.S. labor force will continue to grow through 2015 at roughly the same rate as in the previous decade. After that, the rate of growth in the labor force will begin to slow, albeit not by a lot—two-tenths of 1 percent per year.[17] The estimates themselves are based on some hard measures—how many young people will be moving into the adult ranks in each period; some reasonably solid estimates—how much improvement we will have in life expectancy and trends in immigration; and some pretty "soft" measures. Among the soft and uncertain measures are the labor force decisions that older workers will make. The forecast of a slowdown in the growth of the labor force is based on a slowdown in population growth but also on the assumption that labor force participation rates for the labor force as a whole will actually decline into the future, despite increasing for older workers.[18] To be clear, the U.S. labor force is never projected to decline, although pundits often get that wrong; it is only the rate of increase that is expected to slow. (A good counter to those who worry about an apocalyptic decline in the U.S. population is to point out that the largest high school graduating class in U.S. history was . . . 2008.) Note that these forecasts were based on the state of the world in the early 2000s, before the financial crisis, before the later Social Security age had begun to take effect. If the labor force participation rates for older Americans increase at all, as the arguments above suggest that they will do, then the overall U.S. labor force will expand much faster than even these government forecasts anticipate.

Whether we will have a tight labor market in the future depends primarily on the demand side, on whether the economy will be growing or shrinking. The reason is that changes in the supply side, demographics and the labor force that results, happen quite slowly, with more than enough time to adjust to them. Changes in demand, on the other hand, happen quickly, dramatically, and unpredictably. To illustrate, the United States lost 2.5 million jobs from September through December 2008, while the demographic changes discussed above amount to a change in the labor force of a hundred thousand or so individuals over the course of a year. The ability to predict where the economy will be even a year out, let alone decades into the future, has been dismal.[19]

The 2008 financial crisis, the "Great Recession," is likely to have a longer-term effect on older workers that goes beyond the decline in jobs. Many more older individuals are likely to stay in the labor force—and those who have already retired are likely to come back in—because the declining value of their investments makes it more difficult for them to afford to retire. A 2009 survey of workers age fifty to sixty-four finds over 50 percent reporting that they plan to postpone their retirement three or more years longer than they had expected as a result of the economic crisis.[20]

We can also get some sense of what the response to the effects of the Great Recession will be on retirement plans by looking at what happened after the 2001–2002 stock market slide. The decline in the stock market during that recession of 34 percent was roughly the same as the decline during 2008. As a result of that decline in the stock market, the percentage of people who otherwise would have retired fell by about 2 percent in the following year, and the percentage of people who were retired and came back into the work-force rose by 1 percent. That was a combined 3 percent change in the year following the market decline. If the rates of return in the stock market then returned to their historical level, estimates suggest that retirements would have declined an average of 2.5 percent per year over the next four years.[21] It turns out to be quite difficult to estimate the number of people who retire every year, but for the sake of simplicity, let's say it is 1 million. The 2001–2002 stock market decline would therefore have added 130,000 more older workers to the labor market in the four years after. Because the stock market decline in 2008 was just about the same size, the number of older workers added to the labor force would be roughly the same number as well. The composition of that group of added workers is a little different from the average in that it would include more high-wage individuals as they would be more likely to rely on investment income.

Whether or not the economy as a whole will be up or down in the future, employers will always need workers. And every generation, the pool of workers available to them changes.

There is an entire industry devoted to understanding the special needs and interests of each new younger generation of workers entering the labor force. Dozens of books try to tease out the differences among Millennials versus Generation Y versus Generation X, despite the fact that each one of these groups represents only a trivial part of the total workforce. In contrast, older individuals represent a huge and growing proportion of the population. As we will see later, most of them want to work and are either looking for a new job or looking to recontract employment arrangements with their current employer. They are, as a group, experienced, skilled, and conscientious. Why aren't we paying more attention to them?

The explanation for not paying attention to older workers focuses less on rational calculations of costs and benefits by employers and more on psychological factors, including discrimination. Even if labor markets will be so tight in the future that employers will need all the workers they can get, we know from history that this is unlikely to solve the problem of discrimination. The 1950s and

1960s experienced the tightest sustained labor markets in U.S. history, yet discrimination against women and minorities remained widespread. Economists frequently argued that employers were paying a price when they discriminated by avoiding qualified workers who could be hired at a lower price and that the market would punish them into dropping their restrictive hiring. But it didn't happen. It took political pressure and then social pressure to change the attitudes of the individuals making employment decisions before discriminatory practices began to erode.

Conclusion

Strong external trends—a large baby boom cohort, longer life expectancy, and a higher labor force participation rate—have led to a rise in the number of older individuals. But if older people did not want to work, then these trends would be largely irrelevant for employers. By and large, however, older people want to work, and more of them are likely to want to work longer in the future. They are not motivated as much by traditional rewards (money and the ability to rise in the company rank), but rather place greater value on the "emotional" rewards of work (feeling needed, learning new skills, and contributing to the common good). In the next chapter, we take a closer look at these myths about older workers—and many others—and what emerges is a very different view than the one most employers hold.

2

Myths About Older Workers

The evidence that baby boomers, and no doubt the generations behind them as well, are thinking differently about what has traditionally been seen as the retirement years is overwhelming. They want to work longer, beyond the traditional retirement age, in part because longer life expectancy demands more money and in part because pensions and other forms of retirement income have not kept pace. The National Retirement Risk Index indicates that 45 percent of U.S. households are at risk of not having enough money to support themselves in retirement. This is due in large part to the disappearance of traditional pensions and the modest balances in individual 401(k)s and nonpension retirement accounts.[1] Longer life expectancy and a greater need for money has led to a growing interest in full-time work since the mid-1990s. In figure 2-1, we see that the percentage of older workers working full-time rose from 44 to 56 percent after 1995, while the percentage working part-time fell from 56 to 44 percent. Full-timers now account for a majority of older workers.

FIGURE 2-1

Workers 65 and over by work schedule, 1977–2007

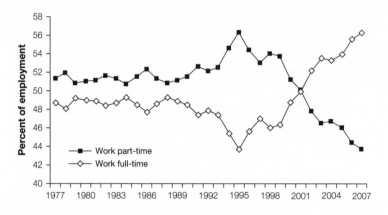

Source: U.S. Bureau of Labor Statistics, http://www.bls.gov/opub/ted/.

The increase in the age to get full Social Security benefits from sixty-five to sixty-seven and the fact that so many workers now have 401(k) retirement plans, which are not funded at the level of more traditional defined benefit plans, will cause both labor force participation rates and the interest in working full-time for older workers to rise well above the current projections because people need the money.[2] And then there is the long-term effect of stock market collapses of the kind we saw in 2001 and especially 2009, which will no doubt send a great many individuals who expected to stop working back into the labor force. Even if 401(k) and other retirement investment accounts come back to the level individuals were expecting, we should anticipate that the financial crisis will lead to some permanent changes in retirement behavior as described in chapter 1. Not just the current generation of older workers but those coming along may be much less likely to rely on investment income alone to support their retirement years. We should expect many of them to want to keep working—or at least keep the options to do so open—as a way to diversify their sources of income in case invest-ment markets turn sharply down again.

Motivation: What Older People Want Out of Work

Given all this concern about money, it may be surprising that older individuals express an even stronger interest in working because they enjoy work, as compared to doing it for the money. Eighty-four percent of those age forty-five to seventy-one say they would work even if they were financially set for life, and 69 percent of that age group plan to work into their retirement years. An AARP study of individuals age fifty to seventy who were still working found that emotional factors—staying mentally and physically active—topped the list of reasons they chose to work (see table 2-1).

TABLE 2-1

Major factors in the decision to work in retirement

Stay mentally active	87%
Stay physically active	85%
Be productive or useful	77%
Do something fun	71%
Need health benefits	66%
Help other people	59%
Be around people	58%
Need money	54%
Learn new things	50%
Pursue a dream	32%

Source: Staying Ahead of the Curve 2003: The AARP Working in Retirement Study, a nationally repre-sentative telephone survey of 2,001 workers ages 50 to 70. The table is based on how 1,020 workers ages 50 to 70, who reported that they planned to work in retirement but had not yet retired, responded to the following question: "Now, I'm going to read you several reasons why some people continue to work in retirement. For each one, I'd like you to tell me whether it is a major factor, a minor factor, or no factor at all in your decision to work in retirement." For each item, the table shows the percentage of respondents who identified the item as a "major factor."

Older individuals who want to keep working don't necessarily want to keep doing the same thing. Many want to try new careers, consulting or working part-time, or start their own businesses. According to AARP, a vast majority (70 percent) are looking for ways to get a better balance between their work and personal lives, in part because many of them are dealing with major life challenges, such as caring for relatives, that pull them away from work. Not surprisingly, flexibility in their jobs was among their top needs.[3]

Why do they enjoy work? More than two-thirds report that they believe their work is making a contribution to society. Whether they changed jobs as they aged or simply focused more on the broader social impact of their work, rewards other than money seem crucial. Work also provides far and away their most important connections to society: ties to the employer are ranked number one and ties to their fellow employees are ranked separately as number three (church and religious organizations are ranked number two) as the most important connections to other people that the respondents reported.[4]

If working longer is a goal, what is it that these workers want to see in a job? The most important factors for older workers in their ideal job are ranked below:[5]

- *Friendly environment:* 94 percent

- *Chance to use my skills:* 94 percent

- *Chance to do something worthwhile:* 91 percent

- *Feeling respected by coworkers:* 90 percent

- *The opportunity to learn something new:* 88 percent

- *Allow me to help others:* 86 percent

- *Feeling respected by my boss:* 84 percent

- *Adequate paid time off:* 86 percent

- *Health care and insurance benefits:* 84 percent

- *Flexible schedule:* 76 percent

- *Chance to do something I've always wanted to do:* 75 percent

Notice that "making a lot of money" is not on their list of priorities. In part, the survey results reinforce the notion that older workers are concerned about schedules and flexibility in how they work. Other surveys of older employees reinforce this point. In fact, most

---

"I Feel Needed"

As we traveled around the country conducting interviews at companies that have been recognized for their excellence in attracting and retaining older workers, we kept hearing the same thing from older workers: why should I stop working when I'm needed and can contribute? Despite the diversity of locations (John Deere in rural Illinois and Roche Pharmaceuticals just outside of Manhattan), industries (Scripps, a health care company, and MITRE, a technology company), and size (L.L.Bean, with a large seasonal population yet a small year-round workforce, and Vanguard, with a large, stable workforce), the older employees expressed remarkably similar views on work. They rarely talked about money or financial concerns, as one might expect. Instead, they almost always talked about those "soft" returns, like feeling appreciated, needed, and respected. Many expressed a strong sense of loyalty to the company and saw their work as a type of legacy. Contradicting yet another stereotype (that older workers are afraid of change), the older workers we spoke to revealed a great interest in learning new skills and growth (both personal and professional). Later on in the book, you will read more about these companies and their strategies for meeting the needs of these valuable employees.

---

older employees report that they ideally want "smaller" jobs that have fewer responsibilities than the ones they had before.[6] A recent study finds that when they change jobs, older workers, on average, shift toward lower-skill but still nonroutine jobs: they may want simpler jobs, but they don't want to be bored.[7]

What is most interesting about this list, however, are the other items. More important than schedules by far, and something that is completely within the control of an employer, is how older workers are treated. The term *respect* features prominently in this list (see "'I Feel Needed'").

Job Performance

The business case for engaging older workers turns on their net value, their contributions minus the costs of employing them. Whether older workers have the skills and experience that employers want won't matter much if they cost more and if they produce less than their younger counterparts. The most important place to begin in addressing that question is on the contributions side: what do we know about the job performance of older workers as compared to their younger counterparts? The reason to begin here is because opinions are strong on this topic and, as we will see, often wrong. The research investigating the effects of aging on behavior relevant to job performance is voluminous. As one might expect, the results can get complicated quickly, although the overall conclusions are remarkably straightforward (see "The Research").

For example, there is a huge amount of variation as to what constitutes *job performance* across different kinds of jobs, but it is probably fair to say that most of our implicit assumptions about job performance are stuck in the industrial era where a worker was carrying out a highly structured task of the kind we might see in factory production work. The key components of good job performance in this context are speed—how many widgets can you turn out per

The Research

Before we jump in to review these studies, it is important to have something like a field guide to the research community that produces them. The incentives for researchers are to find effects in the phenomena they study—in this case, to find differences between older and younger individuals. Careers are rarely built on finding that there are no effects from one's studies, and so researchers studying age seek out contexts where age differences exist.[a] There are also important differences between finding statistically significant effects—the conclusion that the results are most likely real and not due to chance—and the more practical concern as to whether the effects are big enough to have any real importance. Researchers tend to be more interested in the former than in the latter. Most of us see this almost daily with reports that eating this food or taking this supplement either raises or lowers our risk of dying, and we have to read the fine print to see that the actual impact may change our odds of mortality by one-hundredth of 1 percent. Research on aging is often like this. It provides lots of interesting findings about the differences in the mental abilities of older individuals that advance the scientific community's understanding of the process of aging. For readers who are primarily interested in the practical implications for employment, however, the overall conclusion from all this research is that for virtually all jobs in virtually all circumstances, workers with more experience are almost always better performers. Any negative effects of age on performance are so minor as to be irrelevant.

a. The scientific reason for this is that a finding of "no effect" is very difficult to substantiate as there are a great many reasons associated with problems in the execution of the experiment why one might not find a relationship, when in fact one truly exists.

hour—and, to a lesser extent, quality in the form of accuracy. Modern service jobs, where most employees work today, are quite different. The nature of the tasks being performed is much less structured: a customer shows up with a complaint that has to be identified and then addressed, and an important part of the performance of that task is how the customer "feels" about the encounter after. Figuring out the complaint is part of the task, finding a cost-effective solution is another part, dealing with the customer as a person is a third part. And these separate parts may not be equal in importance: the customer may end up satisfied with the encounter, even if their complaint isn't solved, as long as their interaction with the employee was positive. Similarly, they may have their problem solved and still be unhappy because of a bad conversation with an employee. Identifying, let alone measuring, job performance is very difficult in contexts like these.

Assuming we figure out what good job performance means, then we can start thinking about what determines whether we get it or not. We can think of the factors that shape job performance as falling into two buckets. The first one is how the employees are managed, a general issue that gets a huge amount of attention in business and in the press. It gets very little attention in the studies of older workers, however, an issue we focus on in the next chapters. The second bucket has to do with the attributes of the employees themselves. This second category is the focus of virtually all the research around older workers.

Knowledge, Skills, and Abilities

Researchers who study the individual attributes that determine the differences in job performance across individuals focus on three factors as being important: knowledge—what we know about the task and the context where it is performed; skills—reasonably standardized sets of solutions, such as the craft skills of a plumber; and abilities—especially intelligence and other cognitive abilities. In examining the differences between older and younger individuals, the research community has focused overwhelmingly on abilities, largely ignoring knowledge and skills. This is not because abilities are more important in predicting job performance than knowledge or skills. It is in part because it is an easier criterion to apply. Mental ability is a useful predictor across a range of different jobs, whereas knowledge and skills tend to be more specific to each job and are much more difficult to measure. (This is why most employers rely on whether a candidate has done similar work before as a proxy for their knowledge and ability rather than trying to test for it directly.)

In the context of older workers, the unstated assumption is that more senior workers are more experienced and therefore have more knowledge and skills than their less experienced colleagues. This point sounds so obvious that it hardly seems worth noting, which is perhaps the reason that it does not get studied. Yet it is something that is easy to forget once we are immersed in the academic study of older workers. To see that, think how our view would change if we substituted the word *experienced* for *older* in the following contexts: it might seem odd, to say the least, to ask for the oldest doctor in a practice, the oldest carpenter, or the oldest lawyer when we needed help. But it seems obvious that we want the most experienced surgeon operating on us, the most experienced carpenter laying out the addition on our house, the most experienced lawyer handling our estate.[8] In virtually every workplace, employees look to the most experienced workers for advice because knowledge and skill come with experience.

A large number of workplace practices are based explicitly on the idea that skills and job performance are based on experience. The apprentice–journeyman–master career path in craft work is defined by job experience. It plays out the same way in professional services firms (associate–partner–managing director), in medicine (intern–resident–attending), and in the promotion ladders for most white-collar jobs. Seniority-based promotion and pay policies in the business world no doubt serve other functions as well, such as resolving problems of workplace politics, but their acceptability to employers rests on the idea that most experienced workers are better. As noted above, the research in economics is overwhelmingly clear across virtually all jobs in the economy that experience is worth a lot. The word *age* conjures up at best mixed images, while the word *experience* is uniformly positive.

One reason why research focuses on ability differences associated with age, therefore, is that it seems obvious, other things being equal, that older workers will have more experience and therefore have more knowledge and skills. The second reason is that the psychologists who work in this field are interested in ability because it relates closely to issues that are at the heart of important questions in the field of psychology, such as how the brain works. These researchers clearly recognize that knowledge and skills matter, however, and have their own system for thinking about them. Here researchers talk about the difference between *crystallized* abilities and *fluid* abilities.[9] Crystallized abilities are another name for knowledge, the type of information we pick up every day just from being part of society. We might expect that our stock of crystallized knowledge increases the longer we are alive, or at least the longer we are actively engaged in the world around us, and there is support for that view. Whether it continues to rise after that point depends not so much on age per se but on a number of contextual factors, such as how active individuals are.

If crystallized abilities represent concrete knowledge, fluid abilities represent something, well, more fluid, and that is the thinking, processing, and cognitive abilities that are especially important in solving new and different problems. These are flexible in that they can be applied across contexts and problems. We might think of fluid abilities as being associated with what intelligence testing hopes to capture. Most of the tests used to measure fluid ability are timed tests of problem solving, like IQ tests. Fluid abilities rise with age but then hit a peak fairly quickly, in the twenties, and slowly decline.[10] How important this decline is to job performance is an issue we return to below.

Memory seems to be an important component of fluid ability. Perhaps the greatest stereotype about older individuals is that their memories are worse. In fact, short-term memory, the focus of the stereotypes, does not differ much between older and younger individuals. Older individuals who have an illness like Alzheimer's obviously have short-term memory problems, but so do younger individuals with brain-related illnesses. It is the illness, not the age, that is the issue. Increasingly, researchers have concentrated attention on *working memory* as an important attribute in job performance. This is the capacity to store and then use information, exactly equivalent to the notion of random-access memory in computers.[11] Working memory does seem to decline with age, and it does take older individuals longer to solve reasoning problems of the kind measured by these tests.[12]

But working memory is almost never the only or even the most important factor involved in executing work-based tasks. And some of the other relevant factors may actually improve with age. A recent study of airline pilots and their ability to recall commands from the air traffic controllers, for example, found some surprising effects associated with age. These commands are obviously important to remember—"turn left heading 180" has quite a different practical outcome from "turn right heading 180"—and spoken statements are particularly difficult for most people to remember, especially when they are complex and spoken quickly. Prior research found that younger individuals were more able to remember and then execute commands in laboratory settings, in part because of declines in working memory among older subjects. While the researchers in this more recent study found older pilots having more difficulty remembering, they also found that more experienced pilots performed considerably better in actually executing these commands than their younger counterparts. In the context of a real task, the greater experience that older pilots had of listening to and executing air traffic commands as well as their greater knowledge of flight routes more than offset any effects of reduced working memory. One can think of this greater experience as *crystallized knowledge*. And the strong speculation in this context is that the use of simple memory aids, such as a pad and pencil, would effectively offset reasonable age-related memory declines.[13] That would allow the older pilots to perform overwhelmingly better than their younger colleagues, and in practice, pilots are allowed to use such aids.

This result is consistent with other studies of age, experience, and job performance. Neil Charness studied the relationship between age and performance in games like chess, for example, and found that knowledge of the game and its expertise more than offset age-related declines in fluid knowledge.[14] Older workers typically have the knowledge and experience of the work they are doing that helps them perform their tasks well and that can more than offset deficits associated with age-related declines in working memory.

Another set of studies about the age-related effects on performance focused on a specific aspect of job performance: *peak performance,* the exceptional achievements especially in more creative fields like science. The tasks that are the focus of these studies are clearly important, although how paradigm-breaking performance relates to the type of work done in more typical jobs is not at all obvious (e.g., what is required to be an award-winning pianist may have little in common with what is required to be an effective piano teacher). Nevertheless, the results of these studies have generally found that performance peaks in these creative fields in middle age and then declines. What is not so clear, though, is why. Are the declines in peak performance the result of declining ability or declines in other factors, such as motivation—"I've won the Nobel Prize; what's left to do?" The complication with the studies is that age is correlated

with many of the other factors that can explain why peak performance declines. For example, some research suggests that it is not
age per se but the length of time one has been working in a field
that matters.[15] Individuals who have been working in a field for a
long time, for example, can easily get bored with it and lose their
passion. In that case, tenure in the field and motivation are the
issues, not age.

Problem Solving and Adaptability

What do we see when we look at the relationships between age and
actual job performance in more typical jobs? Studies that summa-
rize the relationships between age and performance in actual jobs,
as opposed to laboratory experiments, find that age has little, if any,
effect. Some studies actually find that performance increases with
age, while those that find a decline show only a modest drop-off.[16]
As noted above, older workers might be expected to have more
knowledge than their younger counterparts, which might be com-
pensating for declines in working memory and other aspects of fluid
knowledge. Very few jobs require individuals to perform the tasks
that are most affected by declines in age-related ability—novel reasoning problems, especially under time pressure. Research profes-
sors, for example, solve novel reasoning problems more often than
almost any other occupation, but there are no short-term time constraints in solving those problems. Whether they get solved in thirty
minutes or in a matter of days is completely irrelevant, given that it
takes a year or more to get anything published, as is whether they
are solved with memory aids, seeking help from colleagues, and so
forth. In fact, about the only tasks that fit neatly into the area of difficulty for older individuals are taking the kind of laboratory tests
that psychologists give to assess working memory. So if an employer
has jobs that require employees to take the equivalent of timed SAT
tests every day, changing the questions each time so that they

remain truly novel, then maybe it makes sense to worry about the age of their workforce. Otherwise, forget it.

A different concern one hears about older workers is not about performance per se but the belief that they are not as adaptable to new circumstances and job requirements as are their younger peers. Even if current performance does not differ for older workers, what happens when new challenges come up and they have to do things differently? There may be many aspects to a sweeping claim like this one, but the concern that is arguably most important is the idea that older workers find it more difficult to learn new job-related tasks than do younger workers. Most of the studies looking at age-related learning differences are once again done in laboratory settings and involve solving math-related problems. The results suggest that older individuals take longer to learn how to solve these problems. There is also evidence that it takes longer for older workers to become proficient at new tasks that are more directly job related.[17]

Even in situations like this, though, additional experience can offset the effects of age. When retraining workers of different ages with new word processing skills, the most important predictor of successful performance was prior experience with related software. Older workers without prior experience did worse than younger workers without prior experience—other things being equal, age did matter. When older workers had prior software experience, their performance was no different from that of younger workers with equivalent experience. And older workers with more work experience are more likely to have prior experiences with related tasks.[18]

One really has to work to find evidence about job performance that should make an employer concerned about hiring older workers. Again, the only context where age might matter for performance is where jobs require employees to solve truly novel problems, and the average problem is less likely to be novel for older workers than for their younger peers because older individuals are more likely to have seen or experienced something similar before. It might also be fair to say that older workers take longer to learn or don't benefit as much from training for those jobs that are truly novel to them. But as we saw earlier, employers don't want to hire candidates for tasks that seem novel to them. Nor do they want to train them. They want employees who have done jobs before so that they don't have to make investments in learning or training that gets them up to speed. So as a practical matter, concerns about differences in training required to solve novel tasks are largely irrelevant. All this suggests that in virtually every imaginable work context, employers are better off with more experienced workers who tend, other things being equal, to be older.

It would be interesting to see what the research conclusions would look like if the goal were reversed: rather than looking for the deficits of older workers, what if we went looking for the performance problems of younger workers? In that case, we would be fretting about the difficulties that younger workers have with crystallized knowledge and related factors, which turn out to be the best predictors of job performance. We would bemoan the fact that the deficits in crystallized knowledge are too big to be offset by advantages in working memory, and worry about the additional training that an employer would have to invest in to get younger workers close to the performance levels of their older colleagues. The one advantage that younger workers have, working on truly novel problems, would appear to be pathetically limited in applicability when compared to the deficiencies they face in performing day-to-day tasks and in the newly important areas of emotional intelligence: new workers are almost never given novel problems of any importance to solve. We would be wringing our hands over whether employers could ever be persuaded to hire younger workers. In fact, before the recent concerns about older workers in the labor market, the focus of public policy research was exactly in this area, worrying about the problems that younger workers have in trying to get hired.

More generally, it is hard to see why age-related differences should factor into employment decisions at all. Even if older workers performed worse on some aspect of work performance, it would be foolish to rely on age as a criterion for hiring, because age differences reflect only average tendencies in groups, while the variations across individuals within those groups are huge. To see why this matters, consider by analogy an employer with an unusual job that requires individuals to reach the top shelves in their work spaces. Because of this, the employer decides that it is important as a requirement of the job that workers be tall enough to reach those top shelves. Knowing that men are, on average, taller than women, the employer decides to interview only men for the position. An obvious problem with this position is that while it is true that men, on average, are taller than women, it is not true that all men are taller than all women. There are lots of tall women who could do the job. Gender is a proxy for height, but it is a very imperfect proxy. And there are far better selection criteria to use than gender; the most obvious is simply to require that workers be at least a given height. Further, what about the basic assumption that being tall is required to do the job? Why can't they use a ladder when it is necessary to get to the top shelves?

The analogy with older workers is straightforward. Let's say an employer actually has a job where employees have to solve novel problems, the context where older workers are most likely to have problems. It is true that older workers, on average, are not as good at this as are younger workers (although in this case the difference is much more trivial than the height differences between men and women). But it would be nuts to rule out older candidates, because a great many older individuals are really good at such problems.[19] The appropriate response would be to see how good the individual candidates are at solving such problems—give them a test and see. Especially with job performance, so many other factors—such as education levels, health, and of course prior experience—can swamp any age-related performance differences that it is an enormous mistake to rely on age as a hiring criterion.[20] And just as a ladder might suffice to allow shorter workers to handle the tasks in the above example, simple accommodations—such as allowing workers to use memory aids like paper and pencil or to get help from others—might be enough to make individuals who have deficits completely capable of handling the tasks where they have problems. An obvious accommodation that improves the performance of older workers in almost all contexts is training, an issue we return to in a later chapter.[21]

Cost Differences for Older Workers

Performance differences seem to favor older workers, but do they cost more than their younger counterparts? Knowing whether older workers per se cost more to employ than equivalent, younger workers is a complicated question to answer because age is so closely tied to experience. And experience in a job or even with a company is one of the most important requirements in getting good at what we do, at performance. One of the best-known and consistent findings in the social sciences is that both performance and wages rise with experience, where experience is measured by tenure in one's current job, tenure with an employer, and overall years in the labor force. Employers pay more for experience, and presumably they do so because experience drives better performance. But even here, the difference in pay for experience is not as much as one might think. When we look across the economy as a whole, full-time workers over age fifty-five make about 8 percent more than equivalent full-time workers age twenty-five to fifty-four.[22] The evidence suggests that increases in wages that are associated with age closely track differences in performance associated with age.[23] We can control for tenure in jobs, essentially taking experience out of the picture, to see whether older workers get paid more simply because they are older.

The answer on balance is that they do not. It is only experience that is rewarded in the market, not age. Older workers per se do not cost more.[24]

The old lifetime employment model used to reward tenure per se in part to ensure that older workers always made more than their younger counterparts in the same organization. In the economy as a whole now, the higher wages that used to come with spending more years with the same employer have declined sharply.[25] We can easily see why this would be the case in production jobs: union-based collective bargaining agreements often tied wage increases and promotion prospects directly to seniority or tenure, and nonunion employers often copied those agreements to buy out the interest their employees might have had in joining unions. When employment was lifetime with an employer, seniority and age were highly correlated. Unions have been in sharp decline for at least a generation now, and concessions in the remaining union contracts are widespread. When combined with a decline in lifetime employment, the relationships between age and pay erode sharply.

But these changes have not only occurred in unionized contexts. Researchers studying the semiconductor industry, for example, found a decline in the relative wages paid to experienced workers over time. Among the credible explanations for that change are that new technical skills have become more important, and those skills do not come with experience but typically through higher education.[26]

An implication of the declining rewards associated with longer service, especially with the same employer, is that the cost of changing jobs is now less. Workers who changed employers every other year saw almost the same earnings rise in the late 1980s as did those who kept the same job for ten years.[27] More recent studies have cast some doubt as to how much or even whether the returns to seniority have fallen, but they also suggest that those returns are not very big in any case—roughly 9 percent higher pay for each ten years of additional tenure with an employer.[28] Even these studies suggest that employers no longer place much value on longer service.[29] For our purposes, the idea that older workers are paid more because of longer experience is less and less important. And pay for age per se was never a factor.

Some employers did choose to have pay rise with seniority, but they weren't doing that to be nice to older workers. The higher wages at the end of one's career were offered like a prize or reward for long service. The explanation essentially says that the employer is underpaying them when they are younger, holding back some of their value, like a bond to ensure that they will stick around and work hard through their senior years when the payoff comes. To the extent that this explanation is right, laying off older employees breaks that arrangement and rips off the older employee. Some observers suggest that the main gains that appear to come from hostile business takeovers are funded by cutting the older workers before they can collect on those higher wages.[30]

Experience doesn't have to cost more, of course. In most contexts, it is the market that sets the wages for a job, and not all prior experiences are valued by the market: a retired banker with a forty-year career who does part-time work as a tour guide should expect to be paid like a tour guide, not like an experienced banker. As a practical matter, it should be up to the job candidate to decide whether they will take a job that pays less than they were making or even less than they are worth in some other context. Some people are willing to work for much less because they like the location, they want to try something different, or they just need the money. But many employers are uncomfortable hiring someone who made much more money in a previous position, assuming that the employee will eventually be unhappy with their pay. This approach is presumptuous. It also ignores the fact that our reasons for working may be more complex than simply maximizing our paycheck, and that is especially true for workers around traditional retirement ages. If you call L.L.Bean to place an order, for example, you can find yourself speaking with a retired doctor or accountant. They are certainly not being paid what they made while working in their previous profession, but they choose to be there and are enthusiastic and loyal workers.

Some companies tie other aspects of compensation to tenure. The most prominent examples are additional vacation or sick days that come with greater tenure with the company. A study conducted by Towers Perrin looked at the total compensation costs across various jobs that would occur if an employer doubled the proportion of workers age fifty-five and with over twenty years' experience. In other words, what would it cost if we took the employer's current compensation policies and applied them to an older workforce? Total compensation costs in a typical organization would rise only between 1 and 3 percent, a trivial increase. (It's important to bear in mind that these costs don't reflect the fact that more experienced workers might perform better and be more cost-effective. That is, these are gross, not net, costs.)

They found that the biggest component of that cost increase for an older workforce centered on health-care costs, which account for about 9 percent of compensation. The per-employee cost of medical claims for the over-fifty employees was from 1.4 to 2.2 times greater than the cost of claims for those in the thirties and forties.[31] But there is an important caveat to this estimate of medical claims that may even make older employees cheaper than their younger peers. It is certainly true that older individuals use more health care than their younger colleagues. On the other hand, most employers still offer health-care benefits to employees and their *dependents*. The health-care costs of an employee, therefore, depend not just on their own health-care use but on that of their family. Older employees have fewer dependents because their children stop being covered, in most cases when they hit age eighteen or twenty-two if attending college. While older workers use more health care, their overall family usage is less.

Further, employer-based health-care costs of employees could actually fall after employees reach age sixty-five, because then they are covered by the government's Medicare program. Only 19 percent of larger employers (with more than five hundred employees) offer health-care benefits to retirees who are eligible for Medicare, down from 40 percent in 1993.[32] And these analyses only apply to full-time jobs where employers provide health care at all. Only 5.5 percent of part-time workers in the United States receive health-care coverage from their employer.[33] Unless employers are offering health care to these older workers, the medical costs of older workers are irrelevant to them. Where employers are not offering health care, the additional gross costs of employing older workers are negligible.

In fact, some companies take advantage of the fact that some older recruits already have health insurance from other sources. Vita Needle Company, a maker of stainless steel tubing and (not surprisingly) syringes, actively recruits individuals who have retiree health insurance from previous employers, which makes them cheaper to employ.[34]

Another issue with cost implications has to do with safety, with accident and injury rates on the job. Do older workers have more accidents and injuries? Older workers actually have fewer accidents and injuries than their younger peers, perhaps learning from experience how to avoid them. As one might expect, though, they tend to get hurt worse when they do have an accident.[35] Most accidents at work involve traveling, and the most common of those occur when individuals are driving themselves somewhere. In that context, it is interesting to see what the accident rates look like by age (see figure 2-2). Drivers actually have fewer accidents as they age, although the caveat is that the oldest individuals tend to drive less. While it is true that the very old are more likely to have impairments that affect driving ability, the fact that they drive less means that they have fewer accidents. Perhaps they better understand their limits.

FIGURE 2-2

Accident rates by age

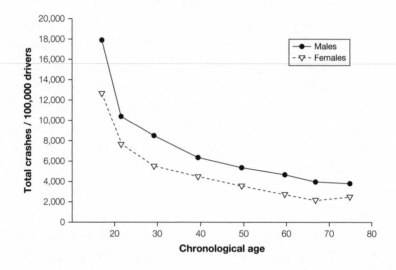

Source: National Highway Traffic Safety Administration, U.S. Department of Transportation, *Traffic Safety Facts 1999,* Table 63.

What can we say about the overall reliability of older workers? Injuries, medical problems, and the distractions of activities outside of work that we might associate with being older could have us think that older workers would be absent more often. The evidence we do have suggests that older workers in fact tend to be slightly less absent—no real difference for women, a negative relationship with age for men.[36]

Days Inns of America did its own detailed study of the employment costs associated with older workers and found that they cost less on four of seven aspects of costs and, overall, cost substantially less than do younger workers. Although the study was done several years ago now, there is no reason to think that the relative costs have changed (see table 2-2).

CVS

CVS recruits mature workers (MWs) through AARP and the National Council on Aging because they stay with the company longer, are good with customers, and provide younger employees with good role models.[a] Older workers are such an important part of CVS's workforce that its director of government programs, Steve Wing, has said, "Without older workers, we wouldn't have a company."[b] CVS is well ahead of the curve on the graying of the American workforce. Anticipating changes in the workforce demographics, the company began recruiting older workers more than a decade ago. Through heavy recruiting efforts, the company has doubled its over-fifty-five workforce, which now represents 16 percent of the company. While some companies, particularly those in retail, use older workers for "light" work, like greeters, CVS has found that older workers are extremely capable across all types of jobs. The company often turns to them to fill positions that require a high degree of organization and discipline. Their attributes also spill over onto their younger workers. "Many older people have a work ethic and sense of civility that the younger generation has not learned yet," says Wing.[c] By having older and younger generations working together, he says, "the older people provide a great example of work ethic and customer service for the young people, and the younger people help to revitalize the older workers and give them enthusiasm for work."[d]

a. Ken Dychtwald, Tamara J. Erickson, and Robert Morison, *Workforce Crisis* (Boston: Harvard Business School Press, 2006), 49–50.

b. Joe Mullich, "They Don't Retire Them, They Rehire Them," *Workforce Management*, December 2003, 49–54.

c. Ibid.

d. Ibid.

TABLE 2-2

Estimated annual employment costs at Days Inns of America

	Younger workers	Older workers
Training[a]	$1,646	$584
Recruiting[a]	96	34
Wages	9,441	9,572
Incentive payments	323	188
Health insurance	674	663
Pensions	28	84
Life insurance	45	48
Total	$12,253	$11,173

Source: William McNaught and Michael C. Barth, "Are Older Workers 'Good Buys'? A Case Study of Days Inns of America," *Sloan Management Review* (Spring 1992): 56.

a. Costs per hire annualized over average length of working career.

Conclusion

When we examine the evidence associated with older individuals in the workplace, what we see is that on virtually every dimension that is relevant to employers, older workers come out ahead of their younger colleagues. Where older workers cost more than their younger counterparts, the gap is relatively small, associated with experience and better performance. Given this apparent advantage, it is worth thinking about what it costs an employer, any employer, to *not* hire older workers. An employer who decides not to consider older job applicants is essentially writing off almost a third of the available workforce and more in the future. What does that cost?

Now that we've examined closely the myths—especially about performance and costs—let's take a closer look at the business case for older workers.

3

New Business Realities and the Business Case for Older Workers

In order to see clearly the opportunities that older workers offer to contemporary employers, it is important to take a moment and look at the human capital challenges that employers now face.

The idea that older workers could be an asset for business and employers generally is relatively new because, as noted in chapter 1, only recently has life expectancy extended enough for individuals to be able to work beyond historical retirement ages. The great U.S. corporations that dominated the world of business through most of the twentieth century were established in a time when age sixty-five was the outside limit of life expectancy. So the career systems they created were based on the assumptions that work beyond that age was neither probable nor desirable. While life expectancy has gradually increased, those lifetime career systems did not adjust, and now they have collapsed altogether.

The Decline of the Traditional Retirement Model

The model for employment that most of us think is the typical or baseline approach actually did not get going until after WWII. After the war, there was a mad scramble for talent as the economy grew quickly and women left wartime jobs to take up traditional family roles. After initial attempts at poaching employees from each other, the dominant approach to managing talent before the war, corporations settled into a model of internal development and lifetime careers for white-collar jobs. For production jobs, unions and the system of labor relations they helped create led to a similar lifetime approach. At least since WWII, the hiring model went like this: Find entry-level workers, recent high school grads for frontline jobs, college grads for management and technical positions. Make investments in them through training, on-the-job experiences, and supervision. Their productivity and performance grew as a result of these investments, and they advanced in their careers "up the ladder" of the organizational chart to positions that required more knowledge, skills, and abilities. In unionized jobs, the promotion paths were tied tightly to seniority; in white-collar and nonunion jobs, the ties to seniority were less explicit but ended up having a similar effect.

It was important for the employer to retain employees in order to recoup the investments in their training and also to have workers with the detailed company knowledge to run these often large and complex organizations. Promotion from within was one way to retain them. Pensions and other retirement plans with vesting requirements—where benefits were lost or at least sharply reduced if one left before retirement age—were another retention tool. Employers also protected employees against job loss when business turned down: even unionized employees, who were routinely laid off in recessions, remained tied to the firm, with employer-sponsored supplemental unemployment benefits that paid them until business picked up and they would be hired back, the most senior first.

This system also explains the logic behind retirement practices. Having a predictable retirement age—sixty-five in most companies—made succession planning and workforce planning easier to do because companies knew exactly who would be leaving the company when. Having executives retire also kept advancement opportunities open, encouraging younger candidates to stick around with a more credible promise of promotion (see "Mandatory Retirement as a Retention Strategy"). And, as noted earlier, when the notion of

---

Mandatory Retirement as a Retention Strategy

Sears, Roebuck pioneered the notion of mandatory retirement as part of its general approach to developing talent. It recognized that part of the cause of its talent shortage was the reluctance of senior executives to develop junior ones. It was asking a lot to have an executive develop someone junior to take over his job, so the company developed mandatory retirement policies in the 1950s to clear out the older executives. T. V. Houser, vice president of merchandising at Sears, Roebuck at that time, said that mandatory retirement was done "entirely to keep the lines of advancement open." Without those opportunities, he noted, the best young managers would leave for other companies: "The very minute they make a mark, some other company begins making overtures to them." Mandatory retirement was therefore ultimately a retention strategy.[a]

a. See Peter Cappelli, *Talent on Demand: Managing Talent in an Age of Uncertainty* (Boston: Harvard Business Press, 2008), chapter 2.

a retirement age of sixty-five began, that age was near the outer boundary of the productive work life for a typical employee. While it might have been possible conceptually to have individualized assessments as to who was fit enough and had the interest to keep working longer, the norms at the time of standardized practices for everyone—advanced not only by unions but through corporate culture—were so strong that the idea never appears to even have been tried.

Given these arrangements, not only was mandatory retirement set at a standard age, but it was counterproductive for an employer to hire older, experienced workers from outside because doing so would essentially take away advancement opportunities from current employees and disrupt the internal model. Pension arrangements made it difficult for older workers not only to leave their current employer (losing that pension) but also to move to a new organization, because they would not have time to build up the years of service necessary to earn a good pension in their new job. Any investments in training and development required to hire older workers and get them ready to contribute would be difficult to recoup because these older hires might not be employed long enough before mandatory retirement to earn back those investments.

Before 1967, it was legal to restrict hiring based on age, and a 1965 study of employers conducted by the U.S. Department of Labor showed that a remarkable 60 percent of the larger companies had explicit prohibitions against hiring anyone over age forty-five, an age that today we do not think is old enough to even count as being an older worker.[1] These employer restrictions also meant that employees had little choice other than staying with their employer until they moved into full-time retirement. Mandatory retirement policies made it impossible to work beyond the retirement age with one's current employer, and most pension regulations made it so difficult and uneconomical to earn money after retirement that almost no one did, even if they could find someone willing to hire them.[2] The promise of the retirement party and the gold watch was the only exit strategy for employees.

Comparative evidence on restrictions against hiring older workers comes from Germany, where laws against such practices also did not exist—in this case, before 2006. A study across all German employers found that despite high rates of unemployment among those over age fifty, the vast majority of employers—75 percent—had no job applicants over age fifty. Presumably, the explanation is that older candidates knew that there was no reason to apply. Of those that did get applications, less than half hired even one older worker. Fully 8 percent of employers had written age restrictions on hiring: no one over age fifty need apply. Of those employers that rejected hiring older candidates or had restrictions that prevented considering them, more than half said that the reason was the limited resilience of older workers, while another 29 percent said that the problem was the lack of flexibility and versatility of such workers.[3] Whether these attributions have any basis in fact is an issue we return to later.

Economist Robert Hutchens examined the outcomes of hiring decisions for older workers across the U.S. economy two decades later, in 1983, well after age discrimination was illegal and the formal policies described above were gone. He compared the situations where older workers were being hired to those where younger workers were hired. Only a relatively small set of industries and firms hired older workers. Younger workers, in contrast, were hired more or less evenly across the entire economy.[4] The industries where older employees were hired tended to be those where investments in employees were less important. That suggested that the traditional employment model, where employers made big investments in employees when hiring them and then recouped those investments slowly over time, was still in place at least in large parts of the economy.[5]

The Contemporary Scene

Whether we like it or not, the whole lifetime career model is pretty much dead, and with it the requirement of mandatory retirement and the prohibition on experienced hires. What killed it was the change in the competitive environment that greatly increased the uncertainty around business plans: whereas companies in the 1950s routinely had ten- and fifteen-year business plans that were followed religiously, most companies today struggle to keep to a one-year plan as markets and customers change their interests quickly, competitors around the globe respond just as fast, and business has to adapt or fail. Much of that adaptation now takes the form of hiring to bring in new competencies quickly in order to change the direction of operations, with the downside of letting go many existing employees whose competencies are no longer needed or who just happen to be in the wrong part of the operation. What has taken the place of the old approach is a new model of a much more open, just-in-time labor market that would seem to be ideally suited to the interests and abilities of older workers.[6]

The move toward this just-in-time model began, or at least became visible, with the sharp recession of 1981, the deepest economic downturn since the Great Depression. Employers moved aggressively to break the lifetime employment arrangements with their employees, and at least initially, the changes had the biggest effect on more experienced workers. The changes began with downsizing, the permanent loss of jobs, and the evidence suggests that the biggest changes were directed first at older workers. The U.S. Bureau of Labor Statistics now defines *long-tenured* workers as those who have been with the same employer only three years or more (a remarkable statement in itself about the erosion of long-term employment relationships), and when we look at the rate at which these long-tenured workers have been permanently laid off from their jobs, those in the fifty-five-to-sixty-four age group had the highest rate of job loss from 1981 to 2000. When we compare them to young workers age twenty to twenty-four, we find that the fifty-five-to-sixty-four age group in fact experienced rates of job loss from 50 percent to twice as great as those of their younger counterparts.[7] In the traditional employment model, where seniority played a key role in determining layoffs and job security, we would have expected that the most senior workers would be the most secure, and the most junior workers would be the most at risk. Now the situation is reversing. The risk of job loss for middle-aged as well as older workers rose relative to their younger counterparts from the mid-1980s to the mid-1990s.[8] Further, the costs of job loss as measured by declines in earnings when finding a new job have grown since the 1980s for older workers who otherwise find it difficult to locate new jobs, even as the improved economic picture saw the costs of job loss decline for other workers.[9] Older job losers are now much more likely to leave the labor force altogether when they are laid off. That is, they give up looking for a new job.[10]

Why have employers been so willing to lay off older workers and break the long-term employment model? There may be several reasons. Perhaps the most important reason for targeting experienced workers in the 1980s and '90s was that companies began to operate differently and no longer needed the skills that had been developed in the previous generation among the now older employees. The best example of this in the corporate ranks was the move away from conglomerate business structures with large centralized headquarters to much leaner, decentralized operations with fewer managers, requiring more entrepreneurial competencies.

There were also economic incentives to do so. Although not layoffs per se, early retirements nevertheless got rid of older employees. They were a less expensive and perhaps less painful way of cutting the workforce because they tapped into existing pension funds that were only available to older workers because of pension regulations. In other words, the costs of the pension buyouts did not land on the employer's current books. A more cynical explanation for targeting older workers is that, other things being equal, those long-term employment models described above made the oldest employees expensive. One explanation for seniority-based payment systems per se is that they represented a way to retain employees over their lifetime: stay around when you are younger and mobile in return for something like a wage premium and pension toward the end of your career. Laying off these older employees breaks that implicit contract and saves the employers a lot of money. Some arguments suggest that the apparent premiums that came from restructuring companies in the 1980s are basically attributable to breaking these contracts through the layoff of older workers.[11]

The nail in the coffin of the old employment model was outside hiring. The flip side of all the downsizing and layoffs has been that companies rebuilt afterward by bringing in new employees from the outside, initially at lower wages than earned by the previous employees. The extent of outside hiring in the United States is quite large: almost 3 percent of the U.S. workforce now changes employers every month, roughly a third every year.[12] A recent study by Taleo, the employment software firm, found that in the large companies that use its software, those we might expect to be the most likely to promote from within, roughly two-thirds of all their job vacancies were filled by outside hires. This is in contrast to studies done in the 1950s and '60s, when the equivalent figure was about 10 percent (internal promotions and assignments accounted for the remaining 90 percent). A recent study of executives finds that 68 percent got into their current job by changing companies, a figure that would have been close to zero a generation or so ago.[13]

To see the rise of outside hiring even in the largest companies that we think of as the models of internal development, compare the careers of top executives in the *Fortune* 100 companies in 2001 to those in 1980 (see figure 3-1). There is a sizable decline in lifetime employees and in years of tenure in the company.

FIGURE 3-1

Descriptive statistics for top executives—career patterns, 1980 and 2001

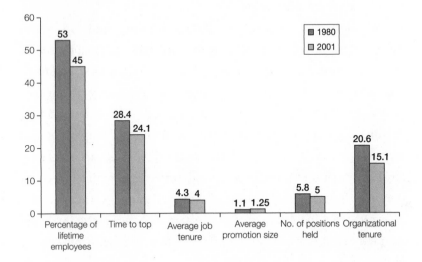

Source: Peter Cappelli and Monika Hamori, "The Path to the Top: Changes in the Attributes and Careers of Corporate Executives, 1980 to 2001," *Harvard Business Review*, January 2005, 25–32.

A related change with special relevance for older workers is that these top executives are now about four years younger than those holding equivalent jobs a generation ago. After WWII, the top executives running the largest companies were in their sixties; by the 1980s, they were in their fifties; now they are in their forties. How having younger leaders running companies might affect corporate attitudes toward older workers is an issue we consider in chapter 4.

The outside hires that employers want are ones who have experience, who can "hit the ground running" in that they can start doing their jobs immediately, without any investments in training and competencies. A study in the late 1990s surveyed recruiters and found a sizable increase in the proportion of employers that now sought experienced workers even for *entry*-level jobs, those positions that traditionally were filled by new-entrant college graduates.[14]

While the downsizing approach caused the most problems for older workers, the demand for experienced new hires that results should also create great opportunities for them. Why that hasn't played out is an issue we consider below.

An important consequence of all this downsizing and outside hiring is that employees do not stay with their employer for long. Many are surprised to find that roughly 40 percent of the U.S. workforce has been with their current employer less than two years. Recent studies using data from the mid-1990s described in chapter 2 find declines in average tenure especially for managerial employees and for the workforce as a whole.[15] The declines in tenure are especially large for older and more experienced employees, perhaps because they had been the targets of downsizing. Figure 3-2, for example, shows declines in tenure for all age groups, but the biggest by far are for men age fifty-five to sixty-four, where it dropped from fifteen years to ten.

For men approaching retirement age (fifty-eight to sixty-three), only 29 percent had been with the same employer for ten years or more, as compared to a figure of 47 percent in 1969.[16]

FIGURE 3-2

Change in median years of tenure, 1983 to 1998, adult men by age

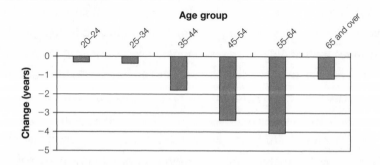

Source: Bureau of Labor Statistics, "Median Tenure Declines Among Older Men, 1983–2000," http://www.bls.gov/opub/ted/2000/aug/wk4/art05.htm.

The percentage of women age thirty-five to sixty-four who spent more than ten years with the same employer actually rose somewhat, from about 30 percent in the 1970s to about 35 percent in the mid-1990s, because women are now less likely to quit their jobs when they have children, in part because of legislated protections. Their tenure has declined slightly since then.

But the overall decline of tenure is not simply a story caused by breaking long-term relationships with older employees. New jobs don't last long, either, even for more experienced workers. To illustrate, the cohort of younger baby boomers changed jobs every two years when they were between age eighteen and thirty-eight.[17] A generation later, when these workers were well into middle age, 40 percent who started a new job saw it end in less than a year; only 30 percent who started a new job saw it last more than five years.[18] Another study compares the experience of men in 1966 to 1981 to those born thirteen years later, during the period 1979 through 1994, when they were the same age as those in the earlier cohort. The odds on leaving a job—being dismissed or quitting—after two years were 43 percent greater in the more recent cohort.[19] Long-term relationships and the investments in them are harder and harder to find.

The fact that jobs don't last long and that employers have targeted older workers in long-service jobs for turnover has helped contribute to the notion of a "bridge job" between the end of a long-term career with an employer and full-time retirement. A Bureau of Labor Statistics study looked at individuals who had a long-term career job (lasting ten years or more with the same employer) and found that about 40 percent of men and 43 percent of women over age sixty had moved onto a bridge job before leaving the workforce completely.[20]

The old objection to hiring older workers (noted above), that they would not be with the employer long enough to pay off the investments their employers made in their training and development, no

Calling Older Workers

Canada's Metasoft, a database company, targeted job candidates over age fifty for its expanding call centers because they stayed with the company longer than did younger employees. Long service in these jobs is important because it allows the employees to develop relationships with customers, which are crucial to sales. In order to attract and keep the older employees, the company also targets them with working arrangements that meet their particular needs. In addition to flexibility in hours of work, Metasoft allows employees with good performance to work from home, an especially attractive arrangement for those with family care or health issues, and 18 percent of the workforce does so.[a]

a. Barbara Jaworski, "IT: Not Just a Young Man's World," Workplace Institute, January 1, 2007, http://www.workplaceinstitute.org/node/23

longer makes sense because nobody stays very long (see "Calling Older Workers"). Overall, older workers are much less likely to quit their jobs than their younger counterparts, although whether that holds true for bridge jobs following retirement from a long-term career and before permanent retirement is unknown. An older worker who decides to keep working for two or three more years is just as likely to be with an employer as long as a new hire straight out of college: older workers may be more likely to leave because they stop working altogether, while new hires are likely to leave to take a job elsewhere. Either way, they are both gone.

The second reason that the old objection to hiring older workers no longer applies is that employers don't seem to be making very big investments in any of their employees. Direct evidence about the extent of investments in training and employee development is remarkably poor in the United States, but what we do know is that training investments overall are not very extensive. Only about 17 percent of employees say that they had any formal training over the course of a year in the mid-1990s, when the most reliable data was collected. That means 83 percent had none.[21] There is some evidence that employers are making substantially fewer investments in new hires now as compared to the past, particularly in the extent of training to learn new jobs.[22] *Training* magazine's periodic survey of overall employer training reported that training expenditures had declined 6 percent in 2003 over the previous year and were below the nominal level of the mid-1990s, not even keeping up with the effect of inflation.[23] Older workers get less training, and those over fifty-five get the least.[24] Deloitte Consulting reports that the average U.S. employer spent about fifty times more in recruiting a typical middle manager than in total in training of its average employee: the focus is on hiring skills, not developing them.[25] Another study, by Towers Perrin, found that while recruiting and retaining employees was ranked a top priority for executives, developing them (other than for executive roles) was ranked the lowest priority.[26] It's simply hard to argue that concerns about the ability to earn a return on training and development represent a significant constraint to hiring older workers. In fact, the apparent decline in investments in employees should make experienced employees who already have skills and experience much more attractive.

Along with the above changes and the decline in the lifetime career model comes the rise of a very different employment model, one that is based on contingent work. The basic idea behind contingent jobs is just that they are not expected to last, but the most important component of contingent jobs is new categories of arrangements that don't look at all like regular employment: part-time jobs, temporary help, independent contracting, and so on. Estimates of the extent of these arrangements are difficult to obtain, but when we look at who is actually working in establishments on a given day, about 15 percent are in these contingent or nonstandard jobs. When we ask individuals to identify their own situation, the numbers are much higher, with 30 percent or more of individuals reporting that their work fits the definition of a contingent job. (Self-reports are higher because many independent contractors or temporary help workers don't have assignments very often.)[27] What employers are after with contingent employment is a just-in-time workforce that is ready to make contributions immediately, that doesn't need to be trained, and that is willing to be brought in and also let go on short notice, in order to respond to uncertainty in the business environment. That definition sounds exactly like what older workers can offer.

One consequence of this just-in-time model and the nonstandard arrangements that go with it is the rise of an "employment services industry" that puts workers and employers together, often for short-term arrangements. This industry itself employed 3.6 million people in the United States in April 2004, with revenues exceeding $100 billion.[28] Unlike most employers, whose real goal is to produce some good or service, these companies are focused on matching people to work assignments. As we will see later, they represent a key piece in the puzzle of how to match up older workers to new jobs.

Changing Skills Requirements

We often hear that the economy is changing in ways that require new skills. The most obvious shift in the past sixty years has been the move away from the hard physical labor of an agrarian and industrial society to the more complex thinking skills associated with the majority of service jobs. Economists Steven Howell and Ed Wolff found that between 1960 and 1985, the loss of unskilled production jobs and the growth in other service jobs led to an overall upgrading of cognitive and interactive skill requirements across jobs in the economy as a whole.[29] Even within production jobs, there was greater demand for higher skills. A study of skills requirements for production jobs in the eight years before 1986 found strong evidence of upskilling in job requirements, combined with some tendency to shift work to those jobs that were experiencing the biggest increase in skill requirements.[30]

Jobs require more skill on average, but which skills are more important? One area where the trends are clear is with the physical demands of jobs, an issue of particular importance for older workers. One of the more common assumptions about older workers is that the physical demands of work may often be too much for them as they age. We consider the abilities of older individuals in the next chapter, but as a point of fact, just how important are physical demands in the modern workplace? An interesting study compared government data on job requirements from 1971 to 2006. In this period, the relevance of physical work and physical demands on workers fell by just about 20 percent. In 2006, only 7 percent of the jobs in the U.S. economy had a high level of physical demands, and a quite remarkable 46 percent of jobs made no physical demands on employees whatsoever. Overall, there are plenty of jobs in the economy—upwards of 80 million—that require essentially no physical strength or resilience.[31]

If physical demands are down, which ones are up? The requirements for interpersonal skills rose by 36 percent, and those jobs that demanded high levels of cognitive ability were up 35 percent over the same period.[32] Sociologist Michael Handel has been investigating the contemporary demands from work across the U.S. economy. He believes that the biggest issues for employers are with "soft" skills associated with interpersonal skills, and cites a survey of rural manufacturers showing that 30 percent of employers reported that their biggest single problem was finding workers with a "reliable and acceptable work attitude." He notes that the "difficulties in finding workers with desired social skills, attitudes, and motivation were often ranked as high as, or higher than, dissatisfaction with cognitive skill levels."[33] This result parallels earlier surveys of the academic skills gap where work attitudes trumped technical skills among employer demands.[34] In other studies, "character" was the applicant characteristic most often given primary importance in hiring decisions by employers (48 percent). Only 5 percent ranked "education" first, and the most common reason for rejecting applicants (other than a lack of prior work experience) by far was the belief that they did not have the work attitudes and behaviors to adapt successfully to the work environment. The most common reasons for firing new hires were absenteeism and failure to adapt to the work environment—attitudinal issues—with only 9 percent of workers dismissed because of difficulties in learning how to perform their jobs, the category most suggestive of a basic skills deficit.[35] A factor that has increased the importance of *work attitudes* broadly defined is changes in the structure of organizations and jobs. Teamwork systems have become more prevalent, making it more important to be able to get along with others and function in a group setting. These skills become even more important because work groups come apart—and also come together—more frequently now as employers churn their workforces through layoffs and outside hiring. Flattening hierarchies reduce the level of supervision and control, and teamwork transfers even more responsibility and decision making to frontline workers. All these developments require that employees make decisions and work out problems along with their coworkers. Interpersonal skills in this context become much more important. Older workers have more experience addressing such problems. A popular phrase used to describe these interpersonal skills is *emotional intelligence,* and a study on emotional intelligence found what we would expect, that the experience that comes with age makes us better at these skills.[36] In short, the competencies that are growing in importance are ones where older workers have an advantage (see "The Mature Staffing Business Model").

The Mature Staffing Business Model

Health Design Plus prefers to hire mature workers from Mature Staffing for stressful, customer service jobs because they have the interpersonal skills and experience, require less training, stay in the job longer, and are easier to manage.[a] Mature Staffing, as its name suggests, is a nonprofit, publicly funded group that helps workers age forty and older find new jobs and acquire new skills. Paul Magnus, the company's vice president of workforce development, believes that its "step-down programs," which allow older workers to ease down from full-time to part-time work, are particularly crucial to manufacturing firms (Mature Staffing is based in Akron, Ohio), which are facing a loss of critical knowledge and skills as their older employees retire. "The older workers can . . . help transfer institutional knowledge to the new workers entering manufacturing," he says. "We help to stabilize the workforce."[b] Another Mature Staffing client, Jim Burns, president of Summit Machine Ltd. in Mogadore, Ohio, says that more than one-third of his workforce is sixty to seventy years old. He says that younger workers do not want a career in manufacturing. "I have truly come to appreciate the older worker," Burns says. "Most of them want to work longer and have a tremendous work ethic."[c]

a. Richard W. Johnson, Gordon B. T. Mermin, and Matthew Resseger, *Employment at Older Ages and the Changing Nature of Work* (Washington, DC: AARP, 2007).

b. Leslie Stevens-Huffman, "Turning to Niche Staffing Firms to Fill Specialized Hiring Needs," *Workforce Management,* March 13, 2006, available at http://www.allbusiness.com/management/3495177-1.html.

c. Ibid.

We often hear the stereotype that jobs today require lots more technical skill than in the past, particularly information technology skills, and that such demands put older workers at a disadvantage. It is easy to assume that older workers just haven't had the exposure to IT systems that younger workers have, but that view is largely myth. IT jobs and IT-related tasks have been around for a long time now. Personal computing and, with it, desktop applications have been prominent in offices since the mid-1980s, and even individuals who are over sixty-five have been around them for decades now. What is distinctive about IT skills is that new technologies render them obsolete quickly, and the new skills do not necessarily build on each other: Knowing FORTRAN programming doesn't help much in learning a newer programming language like Java, for example. So the problem is not that the IT skills of older workers are, over time, obsolete. It is that *everyone's* IT skills become obsolete, and that happens quite quickly, within as few as five years for IT-intensive jobs. While it is true that the IT skills of older workers are likely to be out of date for IT-intensive jobs unless they are retrained, that is likely to be the case for thirty-year-olds as well.[37]

Overall, how do the changing requirements of jobs stack up against the skills of older workers? A sample of HR managers was asked to identify the qualities they most desired in employees. The managers had earlier been asked to assess the qualities of older workers, and the two lists are compared in figure 3-3. The results suggest quite strongly that older workers possess exactly the kind of skills most desired by employers.

Another survey, conducted by Boston College, of employers who employ older workers, reports that the skills and attitudes of their older workers are superior on almost all dimensions (see table 3-1).

Overall, changes in the economy and in the way firms operate seem to be creating much better opportunities for older workers. The lifetime career model, with its mandatory retirements and restrictions on hiring experienced workers, is more or less gone; the new model, with an emphasis on just-in-time employees and contingent work, suits the interests of most older workers; and the changing picture for skill gives greater importance to interpersonal skills and competencies that allow one to hit the ground running. All of this benefits older, experienced workers.

FIGURE 3-3

Human resource managers' ratings for employee qualities

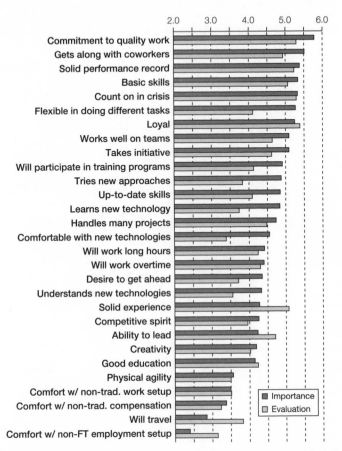

Source: adapted from "American Business and Older Employees" (Washington, DC: AARP, 2000).

The Business Case for Hiring Older Workers

How does all this play out for the individual employer? What is the business case for hiring older workers? The business case depends on the context. The pressure to move more quickly and be more responsive to changing business conditions creates demand for more just-in-time employees. But the problem isn't a shortage of warm bodies or even of fast learners. Employers in this model need to hire

TABLE 3-1

Perceptions of positive workforce characteristics by career stages

Percentage of respondent organizations stating "very true"

	Early career	Midcareer	Late career
Our employees are loyal to the company.	22.4%	37.7%	53.8%
Our employees have a strong work ethic.	24.4%	39.4%	51.9%
Our employees are reliable.	23.5 %	46.1%	51.3%
Our employees have low turnover rates.	19.0%	33.6%	50.3%
Our employees have high levels of skills relative to what is needed for their jobs.	21.0%	38.4%	46.7%
Our employees have established networks of professional colleagues.	16.5%	29.4%	46.3%
Our employees have established networks of clients.	15.8%	29.6%	44.4%
Our employees are productive.	28.5%	42.1%	38.5%
Our employees want to lead and supervise others.	20.4%	33.2%	36.0%
Our employees take initiative.	30.7%	34.5%	32.1%
Our employees are creative.	35.4%	34.0%	29.1%

Source: Marcie Pitt-Catsouphes et al., *The National Study Report: Phase II of the National Study of Business Strategy and Workforce Development,* Research Highlight 04, March 2007, 8, available at http://agingandwork.bc.edu/documents/RH04_NationalStudy_03-07_004.pdf.

candidates who already have the skills and experience to make a contribution immediately. A 2007 study of more than five hundred nongovernmental organizations found that the number one concern for HR managers is recruiting job applicants with the competencies

TABLE 3-2

Competency shortages

Skills	Percentage of respondent organizations answering "yes," skills are in short supply
Management skills	39.9%
Administrative support skills	23.9%
Human resource skills	28.5%
Finance skills	21.4%
Technical computer skills	31.2%
Basic literacy (writing and math)	19.0%

Source: Marcie Pitt-Catsouphes et al., The National Study Report: Phase II of the National Study of Business Strategy and Workforce Development, Research Highlight 04, March 2007, 8, available at http://agingandwork.bc.edu/documents/RH04_NationalStudy_03-07_004.pdf. The survey included 578 nongovernmental organizations with 50 or more people.

they need.[38] The same report pointed to numerous competency shortages facing companies. As shown in table 3-2, management skills (39.9 percent), technical computer skills (31.2 percent), and human resource skills (28.5 percent) are areas suffering the greatest shortages. Both large and small companies report that increased competition for talent led to higher compensation packages and much longer lead times for bringing on new hires, factors that put a strain on quality and customer service and reduced business flexibility.[39]

Three-quarters of executives surveyed by *BusinessWeek* in 2006 report that it became more difficult to find and retain talent in their businesses in the 2000s.[40] A 2007 Robert Half International survey of nine hundred employees and one thousand hiring managers found nearly all (91 percent) reporting that it is equally or more challenging to find qualified candidates and that they could not find enough qualified candidates.[41] A survey of some eight hundred members of the National Association of Manufacturers revealed an extraordinary gap between the supply of skills available and the performance requirements of the workforce needed for modern global manufacturing. These skill shortages cut across industry sectors and impact more than 80 percent of companies surveyed.[42] Another survey found employers ranking "attracting and retaining talent" as a most important priority, while developing talent was least important.[43] The 2009 financial crisis and worldwide recession clearly put a hold on hiring and a damper on the general interest in recruiting, but this time-out is temporary. The problems that led to these shortages—a decline in investments in talent, increased demand for just-in-time skills—have not gone away. And when economies pick up and grow again, as they surely will, the concern about finding enough of the right kind of workers will return.

The bank robber Willie Sutton once explained that he robbed banks because that's where the money is. Employers will need to focus more on hiring experienced workers because that's where the skills are. Among the specific situations where employers find hiring older workers most attractive are the following:

- *Unpredictable and irregular need for employees.* This situation is perhaps the clearest "win-win" in that it represents a good match between the special interests of many older workers and the special needs of the employers. As we saw in chapter 1, the ability to work less than full-time and to have some control over one's schedule is of great interest to a majority of seniors. On the other side, most employers are trying to match their capabilities much more closely to the changing needs of their customers in ways that move them away from the more traditional 9-to-5 schedule. Keeping stores and offices open later, reducing staff during hours when customer demand is less, and ramping up seasonal capabilities or for special projects are all examples.

- *Need for "instant skills."* New companies, in particular, or new locations of existing companies have a great need to get up to speed quickly. It takes time to train new hires how to do their jobs, and if the organizations are truly new, few support systems are in place to help employees learn how to execute their tasks. Businesses that are expanding to new locations now find it quite difficult to use the traditional start-up strategy of moving current employees from the existing operations to the new ones as such moves are increasingly expensive as well as resisted by employees: two-career-couple issues and general concerns about uprooting community and work ties make such moves more difficult.

- *Misjudgment of demand for skills.* Even where employers have internal development programs, they very often misjudge and fall short on the demand for those skills. If it takes a decade for your technicians to truly master their tasks, you have to be able to forecast accurately the demand for those technicians ten years in advance. That is beyond the capability of virtually any employer. Roughly half the time, therefore, they end up with a shortfall, and turning to the outside market for experienced help is about their only option.

How much effort and time employers are willing to spend to attract older workers is closely tied to the difficulty they have in finding candidates to recruit. The nursing and health-care professional shortage, for example, is now well known. The Bureau of Labor Statistics projects that there will be a need for 587,000 additional nurses by 2016.[44] Not surprisingly, health-care institutions are at the forefront of engaging older workers. In fact, five of the ten top companies listed in AARP's 2007 Best Places to Work were health-care companies.

The Business Case for Retaining Older Workers

A different and even stronger business case can be made for finding ways to keep employees who are otherwise planning to retire from one's organization. The core of the case for retaining older workers is similar to the benefits of retaining any valued employee: avoiding the hiring, onboarding, and training costs required to get a replacement up to speed. Estimates of the cost of losing an average employee vary a lot by job but tend to center around the equivalent of one year's salary or compensation for the employee who is lost.[45] Even though older workers will eventually leave, keeping them longer in the same jobs reduces the amount of hiring employers have to do and allows them to economize on all the fixed costs of employment—hiring, onboarding, training, and so forth. Some employees are interested in working in their current jobs longer, and growing life expectancy means that employees should be able to work productively, on average, well past traditional retirement ages.

There is a special urgency in retaining older workers where knowledge retention is an issue. The *BusinessWeek* survey of executives found more than two-thirds concerned about losing "valuable knowledge and hard-to-replace skills" with retirements.[46] In health care, for example, research increasingly points to the fact that keeping individuals and teams together longer improves patient outcomes.[47] When we conducted interviews at Scripps Health in San Diego, for example, several HR managers talked about the costs in terms of patient outcomes associated with losing highly skilled nurses. The outcome of a surgery, for example, depends in large part on the skills of the nurses supporting the surgeon and those caring for the patients when they recover. When complications arise in a surgery, there are always longer hospital stays and higher costs. As a result, Scripps is doing everything it can to keep experienced nurses from retiring, in order to improve patient outcomes (see the Scripps case study in chapter 6). More generally, a survey of one thousand nurses in 2006 found that a staggering 55 percent planned to retire between 2011 and 2020, creating a national retention challenge.[48]

Many organizations have a generation of technical talent ready to retire with no replacements in the works because apprenticeship

Knowledge at Risk at Boston Scientific

During a risk analysis, one of Boston Scientific's small manufacturing plants discovered that millions of dollars in future revenues were at risk if key employees retired before their essential knowledge was transferred to a new generation of employees. Fewer than 25 percent of the critical jobs in the plant had existing employees with the skills necessary to step in as successors. The plant produces woven and knitted textile surgical fabrics for use in treating vascular disease, and there is something of an art to the weaving process. The company set up a program where younger operators worked directly with the veteran employees, many nearing retirement, to learn that art. It set up practice looms and knitting machines for apprentices to practice on under the guidance of the veterans, a step that accelerated learning time by almost 50 percent.[a]

a. MetLife Mature Market Institute and David DeLong & Associates, *Searching for the Silver Bullet: Leading Edge Solutions for Leveraging an Aging Workforce,* November 2007. A copy is available by e-mailing MatureMarketInstitute@metlife.com.

and internal development programs have been cut (for an example, see "Knowledge at Risk at Boston Scientific"). Others have sales forces with customer contacts and connections that will be lost when they leave. Some extreme examples can be found within U.S. government agencies. NASA, for example, in contemplating the current plan to return to the moon in the next decade, is essentially starting over again as many of the engineers who worked on the Apollo program in the 1960s have either retired or died, taking with them much of the knowledge about how to get there. The program is estimated to cost taxpayers $100 billion.[49] Similarly, the FBI has seen a wave of retirements, leaving the agency with a higher proportion of inexperienced agents: more than 40 percent of its 11,400 agents have five years' or less experience on the job.[50] The FBI contributed to the problem by having a mandatory retirement age of fifty-seven. Other industries facing severe brain drains include utilities (including oil, gas, and electric companies), where about half of the four hundred thousand power industry workers in the United States are eligible to retire in the next five to ten years.[51] At the same time, power demand is expected to increase by 50 percent in 2020, and utilities are planning to open hundreds of new plants and thousands of miles of new transmission lines.[52] This perfect storm has left utility companies scrambling to fill positions.

The full costs of lost knowledge are hard to quantify, but a detailed effort to outline the most important costs has been done in the context of law firms.[53] Here are the costs when a typical lawyer leaves: lost productivity (calculated at 50 percent of the person's compensation and benefits for each week the position is vacant); the costs of the training the firm provided and will have to replicate in a new hire; the costs of lost knowledge, skills, and contacts the departing lawyer takes with him or her; the costs of stopping payroll and other administrative costs; and the effect of high attrition on the morale and productivity of the attorneys who remain. Then we have the host of costs that kick into place when a replacement attorney is hired. They include recruiting expenses and headhunter fees, hiring or signing bonuses, bar and moving expenses, interviewing time spent by lawyers at the firm, and the reduced productivity costs of an inexperienced attorney. The total of all these costs was typically several times the cost of employing the lawyer for a year.

A study of organizational "forgetting" published in the *MIT Sloan Management Review* noted that the loss of organizational knowledge when employees leave is costing companies millions of dollars every year. "Lost knowledge means forsaken capabilities and potentially decreased competitiveness," write the authors. "When a company finds itself in the situation of having to reinvent or buy knowledge it once had, resources are wasted." What's more, tacit knowledge, the kind of unwritten knowledge one accumulates over time, is now understood as an important driver of innovation because of its ability to help with problem solving, problem finding, and prediction and anticipation.[54] Often, the tacit knowledge cannot be recovered.

Some companies are trying to head off these problems of lost knowledge associated with employees retiring before they occur. Chevron, for example, requires all of its operating units to conduct an annual demographic analysis or audit to identify potential talent shortages. Central to the audit is analyzing patterns of retirement—who will be leaving when, and what crucial skills and knowledge might they have?[55] But most companies are doing little. Despite the concerns about losing the knowledge that older employees have when they retire, only 14 percent of U.S. executives surveyed reported that their companies were very committed to retaining employees who were about to retire, and only a third were even trying to quantify the costs of turnover.[56]

One reason may have to do with a lack of mechanisms for retaining knowledge. Under the lifetime employment model, a successor was typically assigned to shadow a retiring manager or another expert employee for a year or more to learn the latter's tacit knowledge in the context of doing the job. This model was incredibly expensive as it effectively meant paying two people to do the same job for a year or more. An alternative approach is to try to grab all that knowledge before employees retire. Australian bank Westpac piloted a program in which certain older workers, defined as "sages," worked with a facilitator to identify their tacit knowledge—the kind of knowledge that isn't in policy manuals but that one gathers over time—before they retired and then post the material on the company's intranet.[57] For most jobs, however, it is impossible to know in advance what knowledge is at risk of being lost (the catch-22 here is that one has to more or less know what the knowledge is to understand whether it is at risk), and attempting to capture it all in advance is a huge undertaking.

Much better than either trying to pay two employees during the knowledge transfer process or trying to copy down all the knowledge in advance is to maintain relationships with the employees who are about to retire, keeping them on as mentors, consultants, or experts so that the knowledge can be passed along when it is needed. The advantages of this approach are, first, that it is open ended. A successor can ask for advice and help when the need comes up, on a just-in-time basis. Knowledge transfer isn't constrained to a fixed succession/transition period. Second, it is much cheaper than the old model because the retired employee is being paid just for the knowledge transfer help, which is much less than full-time.[58]

Retaining knowledge by maintaining relationships with employees who would otherwise leave does not necessarily require that the retiring employees stay in the same jobs that they held before. Being able to call on them when needed may be enough. Argonne National Laboratory offers a classic example of this situation in that most of the work it does requires government security clearances, which can take a long time to secure. It encourages retiring employees to join Argonne's *special term appointees*, those with specialized professional and technical knowledge, and security clearances, who can fill temporary positions.[59]

Some of the situations where retaining employees who would otherwise retire, either in their existing roles or with alternative relationships, is crucial include the following:

- *Where lead times are long and unpredictable.* Industries like pharmaceuticals or petroleum development may have projects that take twenty or thirty years to develop and bring to market. The specific knowledge of the project and especially its history is very difficult to replicate. Such projects rarely have a predictable completion date—drug development, for example, is almost impossible to predict. It can be a disaster in such circumstances to have an employee retire when the project is still in its crucial stages, taking all that tacit knowledge with them out the door. And planning in advance when to transfer what knowledge doesn't work well, because it is almost impossible to predict the progress of drug development.

- *Where company-specific knowledge is crucial.* An example comes from John Deere, which recently branched out into data services that complement its equipment. There is no software that matches up its equipment to the agricultural challenges, so it has to develop its own wind farm, crop-watering patterns, and other software. The engineers who are developing the software need to have deep knowledge about the company's products in order to develop these new systems. Deere uses retirees to help with some of these new product launches.

- *Where culture needs to be solidified.* Organizational culture represents the norms and values, often unstated, that tell people how to behave. One of the most important factors affecting the culture of an organization is its internal demography. Bringing in a lot of new hires, especially experienced hires who have worked elsewhere, means adding people who not only know little about the company's culture but come in with their own norms and values that were established elsewhere and rarely fit the new company. When this is combined with a rapid exodus of experienced employees, the company's norms and values can shift quickly. Retaining older employees is one way to stabilize the culture in the face of outside hires, especially when a company is bringing in lots of new hires. Older, experienced workers are particularly important in passing along the culture because the new hires look to them to figure out how to behave and what to do. Intel partners older workers who have long tenure in the company with young and new hire employees for six to nine months to transfer culture and tacit knowledge about the company: the pairs go to class together and set up a contract stating the goals of the partnership.[60] RBC Financial Group does something similar with teams of older executives and rising managers to transfer company values and culture and tacit knowledge to the next generation.[61]

Northrop Grumman works on this problem of transferring culture in an especially creative way. It engages its retirees to run seminars to teach new hires about the company and its business. (Many companies try to get their current executives to perform these tasks, but they are overwhelmed with other demands and often brush them off.) The retirees have the benefit of an even longer view of the company and its history than most current employees, something that is especially important for understanding company culture.[62]

- *Where demographic balance is needed.* Many organizations end up with a peculiar demographic profile because they grow in spurts, hiring young, entry-level workers disproportionately at different points in time. A company that boomed twenty years ago, for example, is likely to have lots of employees in their midforties now. The demographic profiles that result can have big impacts on the way companies operate, as they shape the profile of experience among the employees. We know, for example, that younger employees with less experience take greater risks. In financial markets, younger employees who have not lived through cycles in markets will think very differently about their decisions than those who have seen them. In such contexts, it is especially important for companies to retain older employees and incorporate them into important decision processes to moderate the risk-taking profile that would otherwise emanate from a young workforce. One of us asked the prosecutors of the Enron executives what struck them overall about that troubled company after having spent a year or more digging into the transgressions of its leaders. One of them said, "I thought to myself, where were the adults in this company? Where were the old hands to tell all these young executives that what they were doing was crazy?"

- *Where younger workers need training.* Employees learn a great deal from each other, arguably more than they learn from training programs or even from supervisors, because the learning takes place on the job, in the context of performing the tasks that matter. In order to train the next generation, as well as to stave off nurses retiring because of the physical demands of the job, Scripps Health created a new position, clinical nurse mentor, to allow experienced nurses to mentor younger nurses at the bedside. With this new role, the clinical nurse mentors do on-the-job instruction while the new nurses do more of the "heavy lifting" of clinical nursing, effectively splitting the role and incorporating learning in the process.

- *Where managers need mentoring.* The complex process of developing individual employees into leaders of their organizations is typically done in the context of supervising and managing, and the key challenge is to learn from those experiences. Mentoring offers the insights of more senior and experienced managers to help those with less experience make sense of work-based challenges as well as something like "coaching," real-time advice as to how to improve outcomes. Many companies, like Dow Chemical, are formalizing the mentor process by assigning protégés to older executives, who serve as mentors.[63] The difficulty with this approach is to find current employees who have the experience, the inclination, and especially the time to be mentors. Union Carbide took the idea of older mentors a step further, using its retired executives to act as mentors to younger executives.

Using retirees in the above roles may be an attractive alternative to trying to retain older employees longer in full-time jobs. Among other things, the older workers may want to move on—we can't expect to solve the knowledge transfer problem by having them stay forever—and keeping them in their current roles impinges on advancement opportunities for less senior employees.

Yet there remains a great deal of resistance to employing older workers and especially to managing older workers with arrangements they might prefer in order to keep them in the labor force. The most telling results may be those presented earlier, that managers' biggest concerns about employing older workers have to do with the potential for conflicts with younger workers; the other important finding is that what older workers want most, and presumably aren't finding, concerns respect. In the next chapter, we deal with those issues head-on, as they may be the single most important constraints to making better use of the older workforce.

PART TWO

Managing the Older Worker

4

Confronting Ageism

As we saw earlier, older people want to work. Employers generally have positive things to say about their own older workers and see them as a source of advantage for their business. The evidence in chapter 2 shows definitively that they perform better on virtually every relevant measure of performance, and cost differences are at best trivial. And as we saw in chapter 3, keeping older workers engaged longer, even if in different arrangements, is a necessary part of the solution to retaining knowledge; and hiring new ones offers the just-in-time workforce that employers say they need. Given this overwhelming business case, it is hard to understand why older workers face so much resistance in getting and keeping jobs. Something must be happening at the point where the employment decisions take place.

And that "something" is age discrimination. A full 67 percent of individuals age forty-five to seventy-one in an AARP/RoperASW survey said that they had seen or experienced age discrimination in the workplace. Fifteen percent reported that they were denied a job based on their age, 9 percent claimed being passed over for a promotion, and 6 percent said they were dismissed (laid off, fired, or forced out) because they were older.[1] If it seems incredible that a compelling business case could be overwhelmed by the attitudes of individual managers, remember that the same thing happened with gender and race.

Attitudes Toward Older Workers

Employers are only human, of course, and like almost everyone, they tend to like people who are similar to them; younger people tend to think more highly of younger people, while older people think more highly of older people.[2] An individual who is different from the person evaluating them—older, for example—will be at a disadvantage, compared to those who are more similar to the evaluator. Beyond the similarity factor, individuals also hold stereotypes associated with different ages. The stereotypes about older workers tend to sound reasonably positive across all age groups. It just so happens that the stereotypes of younger workers, on balance, are even more positive, which places older individuals at a relative disadvantage.[3] There is some evidence, unfortunately, that the group most likely to hold negative attitudes toward older adults is actually other older workers themselves.[4] The group that has the greatest preference for younger individuals is the middle-aged (the group also most likely to be bosses).[5] Why that is remains a subject of debate, but one suggestion is that middle-aged and older employees may feel a greater need to pick up and apply the biases of their organizations in order to fit in, perhaps as a means of indicating that they are not part of the disparaged group. The most common negative stereotype of older individuals is that they are less adaptable than their younger counterparts, a bias that extends across cultures.[6] These work-related stereotypes continue past the traditional retirement age. Employers see retired workers as more likely to lack the appropriate skills and the ability to be trained.[7]

Most individuals with any degree of social awareness know that it can at least be risky to express openly disparaging views about

groups in society. Simply because someone says they are not prejudiced, for example, is no proof that they are not. (Indeed, those who
go out of their way to deny prejudice may well be overcompensating
for their discriminatory attitudes.) To get a more accurate measure
of the true extent of discriminatory attitudes, a group of researchers
has been using a more indirect method of measuring individuals'
implicit or unstated attitudes. This approach shows subjects traits of
individuals—some good, some bad—and then asks them whether
that trait is, for them, associated with various groups. More subtle
still are tests that rely on the speed with which we make associations:
it is easier and faster for us to make associations between traits and
groups that we already have thought about and believe than to make
associations that contradict our underlying views, so sophisticated
tests can reveal which traits we associate with what group based on
how quickly we make them. The most famous of these studies have
been directed at race. But more recently, they have turned to age.
And the negative biases they discovered toward older individuals
were the biggest yet, bigger by far than racial bias. What's especially
interesting about these results is that even the explicit attitudes
toward older individuals—the ones stated out loud—are negative.

While it is possible in studies of other biases to treat the group you
are not part of as some "other," and therefore to be more negative
toward them, it is very difficult to imagine (unless you are Peter Pan
or Roger Daltrey of The Who) that you will never get old. Remarkably, older individuals taking the test themselves report that they
identify more strongly with younger people than with their own
older age group.[8] Explicit biases against age decline as we get older—
no surprise there, as we might think it is harder to express biases
against "people like me." But interestingly, the implicit, unstated
biases do not decline even as we get older. (To take the test yourself,
go to http://implicit.harvard.edu/implicit/.)[9]

What employers say about older workers per se seems to be quite
supportive of the value they get from their own older employees.

How May I Help You?

The survey results discussed in this section, showing that older workers tend to be better with customer interactions, were confirmed by
our company interviews. Customer service is of particular interest to
L.L.Bean, a company that is considered the gold standard for customer
service. L.L.Bean relies heavily on older workers to fill in during peak
season, when its fifteen hundred employees swell to six thousand.
Martha Cyr, vice president, human resources, says that older employees "understand what outstanding customer service means."[a] She also
uses words like *common sense, loyalty,* and *knowledge* to describe the
benefits of older workers. An added benefit, says Cyr, is that the strong
work ethic displayed by the company's older workers serves as a model
for younger employees, who are still learning what it means to be part
of a workplace.

a. Martha Cyr, interview with author.

A 2006 survey of employers, for example, found 88 percent reporting that the "valuable knowledge" shown by mature workers was a
source of advantage for their business, with 74 percent reaching the
same conclusion about the reliability and dedication of older workers.[10] Another survey of employers, also in 2006, found that older
white-collar workers were substantially more productive than their
younger colleagues. Older workers were overwhelmingly seen as
more knowledgeable and better at customer interactions (see "How
May I Help You?") Surprisingly, about twice as many employers in
this survey thought that older workers learned new tasks faster than
younger workers, despite the common stereotype that they are less
adaptable. Older workers were seen as more expensive, but in terms
of overall value were viewed as a little better than younger workers

in white-collar jobs, and about the same for other positions.[11] And as we saw in chapter 2, the actual cost differences for older workers are trivial, arguably more than offset by performance differences. A majority of employers in a third 2006 survey reported that older employees were more loyal, were more reliable, and had a stronger work ethic than younger workers.[12] Whether the positive attributes were attributed to years of experience rather than age per se may not matter much in practice because the two go so strongly together, but it does complicate that argument conceptually.

These reports may be a bit like others that have a self-serving bias—my kid's school is fine, but schools as a whole are bad. And employers are not uniformly positive even toward their own older workers. As with the other research cited above, employers believed that older employees were less creative, and a nontrivial percentage across all the surveys believe that older workers have more trouble learning. Some report concerns that research clearly refutes, such as the belief that older workers are less healthy or that they will not stay on the job as long.

Far and away the biggest concern about older workers, reported by 88 percent of respondents in one survey, was not in fact a problem with the older workers themselves but a worry about conflicts in the workplace with younger workers.[13] And the punch line is that despite the overall positive attitudes toward their older workers, one-quarter of employers reported that their organization was reluctant to hire any older workers.[14] We return to this important issue in chapter 5.

The complaints by employees seem to come especially when employers think about hiring "other" older workers, not the ones they already have, and to a lesser extent when contemplating extending work to their current employees beyond retirement.[15] The problem this creates for older workers is that the layoffs and churning of the workforce described in chapter 2 mean that many, and perhaps most, older workers at some point will have no choice but to find new jobs if they want to keep on working. They aren't always able to keep working for the same employer that knows and appreciates them. Some will also need to change employers in order to relocate, to pursue different kinds of work, or to work different schedules. Even those who want to keep working with their same employer beyond the usual retirement age will have to be "rehired" in the sense that their employer will make a decision as to whether to bring them back in a new relationship. The ability to keep working depends on whether employers will hire or retain them, and that depends on what employers think about the value of older workers.

Self-Reports of Employer Age Discrimination

More interesting than what employers say or even think about older workers is what actually happens in the workplace. Self-reports of employer discrimination against older workers are widespread, as noted above. These are big numbers. It's certainly possible that these reports overstate the true extent of discrimination—it's easy to attribute a bad outcome at the workplace to bias, when the true cause lies with the individual's ability or performance. But it's revealing that the respondents thought that age discrimination was substantially more prominent in their situation than was gender or racial discrimination.[16]

And how old does one have to be for age discrimination to begin? A survey of senior executives in large companies, who are themselves among the oldest employees in their organizations, finds more than 60 percent reporting that it was apparent between age fifty and fifty-five (see table 4-1).

Another measure of the extent of discrimination against older workers is to look at formal charges brought to the government's main watchdog on these matters, the Equal Employment Opportunity Commission (EEOC). These charges may not be a completely accurate measure of the extent to which discrimination takes place

TABLE 4-1

Age at which age discrimination becomes apparent

Age 40	3.4%
Age 45	16.0%
Age 50	36.5%
Age 55	24.6%
Age 60	10.0%
Age 65	2.0%
There is no age discrimination	7.5%

Source: The Association of Executive Search Consultants. Sarah E. Needleman, "Overcoming Age Bias at Work: A Look at Personal Finance Trends and What They Mean to You," *Wall Street Journal Online*, December 5, 2006.

in the workplace, because bringing such cases requires a fair amount of effort, and the potential benefits of doing so vary a lot depending on the circumstances. For example, in 2008, when the economy was sliding into recession and finding new jobs was more difficult, charges of discrimination jumped 15 percent over the previous year. The increase in charges of age discrimination per se in that period rose almost twice as fast, just under a 30 percent rise. Over a longer period—from 1998 to 2008—complaints of discrimination based on age rose from 19 percent of all discrimination claims to 26 percent.[17]

Economist David Neumark's analysis of formal complaints of discrimination brought to the EEOC finds that complaints about unfair discharges are by far the most common category of age discrimination, and that is true for discrimination based on race and gender as well. Other aspects of discrimination may be more common—day-to-day harassment, for example—but losing one's job is such a costly and disruptive event that it is worth fighting it, which is no doubt why it shows up as more common in government statistics. While charges of discrimination in hiring are much less common, again in part because the damages are lower and therefore less worth the fight, they nevertheless account for twice as many of the age-based complaints as compared to race and gender charges.[18]

Other Evidence of Negative Bias

The best bet for an older worker who wants to keep working is to do so with their current employer. But that is becoming more difficult to do. A survey of employers in 2002 looked at age-related employment practices that might make it easier for older individuals to work beyond the typical retirement age. Only about 14 to 16 percent had policies that allowed older workers to reduce their hours of work and still keep their jobs, although informal or discretionary arrangements for doing so seemed to be more widespread.[19]

A review of all the research studies examining age effects in performance appraisals and other forms of work-based evaluations finds a negative bias against older workers. The overall effect is small, but it is still negative. Other things being equal, older workers tend to get worse evaluations. This is despite the fact that the most careful research on the topic of actual productivity, as opposed to supervisor evaluations of performance, suggests that older workers are more productive than their younger counterparts.[20] The good news is that when one looks at the results over the years, that bias has declined, so that older workers are less likely to get negative evaluations now as compared to earlier periods.[21] One would hope that the explanation for the decline in the negative relationship over time represents a decline in prejudice and stereotypes, but we cannot know for sure. We examine this problem in detail below.

In organizations where employees report evidence that employers have preferences for younger workers, older employees get fewer promotions, see less growth in their wages, and are more likely to quit. It's certainly possible that some of these responses result from self-serving biases—I was passed over for a promotion, so the employer must be biased against people like me. But these results hold up even with attempts to control for such biases.[22] An investigation of working arrangements for older workers in Europe found disturbing patterns in practices that affect the long-term situation even for those who were employed. For example, older workers were less likely to be working in teams, thereby increasing social isolation and reducing the ability to learn from others. They were much less likely to get training, and those over fifty-five were the least likely to take training or education courses. Their jobs were less likely to offer opportunities to solve new problems or learn new things.[23] Such situations can easily lead to a vicious circle where employees become disengaged and employers stop investing in them.[24]

But the biggest problems seem to come when older workers lose their jobs, as they increasingly do. Workers over fifty are now more likely to lose their jobs than their younger peers, reversing the historic norm of "last-in, first-out" layoffs, and the rates of job loss for older workers have been rising steadily.[25] How do they lose their jobs? With few exceptions, mandatory retirement programs are illegal in the United States.[26] But other factors can affect whether individuals can continue in their job. Nancy Ezold is an attorney whose practice handles only discrimination cases. She sees a pattern to the way in which age discrimination leads to older employees being dismissed. In a large proportion of these cases, the change that leads to discrimination is the arrival of a new, younger manager. Then she sees three new developments. One is a sudden change in "performance." As she describes it, "An employee in their fifties or sixties, with maybe thirty years' experience, is all of a sudden rated as unsatisfactory. When you tell a worker who is fifty or sixty who has been performing well that they're not doing well, it's absolutely devastating." This is a prelude to being able to fire them for poor performance.

The second development is to "manage the person out" to get them to quit. Supervisors, she says, "have to make a paper trail, so they start micromanaging the person, make the person's life miserable, send e-mails saying you didn't do this right, you didn't meet this goal, start raising goals (often sales) above and beyond anything that the person's peers have to meet." Another sign that this process is under way, she says, is to take away responsibilities, humiliating them in front of their peers, and stop inviting them to conferences and meetings. The third development is to be assigned to "special projects." "This is another, almost a sure sign that you are being pushed out," says Ezold. "The special project serves to isolate you, take you out of the mainstream (not a professional track); you report to one person and no one reports to you, and when the special project is done, the job you had is gone."[27]

When they lose jobs, older workers remain laid off longer than their younger counterparts—twenty-six weeks, on average, versus nineteen for younger workers. And when they do find jobs, they suffer bigger cuts in pay than their younger peers. One estimate suggests that about 13 percent of older job seekers have over the years been so discouraged by the difficulty in finding a new job that they give up and withdraw from the labor force altogether.[28]

Outright Bias in Hiring

The biggest problem for older individuals is to persuade a new employer with which they have no prior experience to hire them. A number of hurdles are thrown in their path even to be able to apply for jobs. For example, a common recruiting tactic with an adverse effect on older workers is "experience-limiting job requirements," specifying, for example, that a position requires five to ten years of experience and not more. No one with more than ten years' experience need apply, and those in that category just happen to be older. Why would anyone not want a candidate who is more experienced? When jobs were defined much more narrowly, it was common for applicants to be told that they were overqualified for a position, the concern being that they would become bored or frustrated with the limited requirements of the job and quit. In most organizations now, the concern is the opposite, that jobs have greater scope for contributions than the individual candidates can muster. So there is a clear upside to having workers who are more qualified for the immediate requirements of a job. And turnover is so common—employer restructuring that shakes up jobs, employees moving on for better opportunities—that the previous fear that a candidate might not be making a lifetime match seems quaint.

In this context, it seems much more reasonable to simply be realistic with candidates about what the job is and let them decide whether it is a fit for them. Indeed, many of the HR managers interviewed for this book say they believe that older people tend to make very good decisions when choosing jobs; they know very well which jobs suit them. Perhaps it's because they have had enough experience to know themselves and the kind of work that will appeal to them. Finally, experience-limiting job requirements are discriminatory unless the employer can show—with evidence to back it up—that applicants with more experience won't succeed in the job. A hunch isn't enough.

Studies from Australia offer evidence about how job requirements can limit hiring older workers. When looking at a representative sample of job advertisements in that country, researchers found that 44 percent were targeted at candidates in their twenties and another 49 percent pitched to those in their thirties or below. Only 6 percent seemed open to candidates over age forty. A study of Australian staffing firms found 27 percent saying that their clients, the employers, preferred not to hire anyone over age forty-five. Yet another study reported that almost a third of Australian employers asked candidates about their age, a practice that is illegal.[29]

The fact that we can see outright bias in hiring is perhaps especially remarkable because it is so clearly illegal. In the United States, the Age Discrimination in Employment Act of 1967, amended and extended in 1978, provides the clearest and most comprehensive regulations against discrimination of any of the regulatory efforts to remove biases against protected groups. It protects individuals over age forty, including job applicants, from discrimination in all aspects of employment—hiring, pay, benefits, job assignments, training, and so forth. An employer that wants to restrict jobs to younger employees must have what is known in legal terms as a *bona fide occupational qualification*—in other words, clear evidence that age matters not just to the job but to the essence of the business or organizational goal. The Older Workers Benefit Protection Act of 1990 extended protections to prohibit employers from denying employee benefits, such as health care, to older employees when they offer them to younger employees. State legislation extends protections but cannot undercut these federal requirements. The Equal Employment Opportunity Commission is a separate federal agency that enforces these acts, and many states have equivalent agencies to enforce state-level regulations.

What all this means in practice is that employees who feel that they have been discriminated against on the basis of age can take their complaints directly to these agencies. They do not have to hire a lawyer to take up their case. Few employers that have dealt with these agencies on age discrimination cases report that it was a fun experience even if they win the disputes, which explains why most employers try to avoid discriminatory practices. Passage of the 1990 act has been shown to have increased the employment of older workers.[30] Virtually all developed countries now have legislation prohibiting discrimination against older workers and agencies to enforce them.

One would think that with such legislation protecting older workers against employment discrimination being so prominent, it would be difficult to find examples of explicit bias in hiring. But in fact they are easy to find. The most revealing evidence about age biases in hiring in the United States comes from a pair of studies where employers were the unknowing subjects of experiments. In the first of these, employers advertising job openings were sent applications from two pretend candidates. The résumés of the two candidates were essentially identical except for their age. The younger candidate was about 44 percent more likely to be offered an interview, the next step in the hiring process, than the older candidate. The researchers found that each additional year of age lowered the chance of the older candidate being called back for an interview by 4 to 7 percent. A candidate who was ten years older had less than half the chance of being called back than did their otherwise identical peer. (Interestingly, in one location the rate of acceptance for interviews actually increased somewhat for individuals over age fifty-five. That location? St. Petersburg, Florida, the place many see as the retirement capital of the United States.)[31]

The second study was even more blatant in that it actually sent two applicants who were otherwise identical except for their age to apply for entry-level sales and management jobs around Washington, D.C. The older applicant got less favorable responses 41 percent of the time, a difference almost identical to the résumé study above. In three-quarters of the cases, the older candidate was rejected before they could even present their qualifications. Typical of the difference in treatment was where the boss of a vacuum cleaner store offered the older candidate a part-time position "until you feel comfortable with sales," while the younger partner got a full-time position. Where both candidates were offered positions, the older candidate was offered lower-value health insurance in one-third of the cases. Controlling for other factors, the study showed that the older candidate faced discrimination one-third of the time for sales positions and an amazing 100 percent of the time for management positions.

The study also explored what happened when the paired applicants worked through employment agencies. We would think that these agencies would be reasonably unbiased and simply reflect the preferences of their client employers. Yet here the rate of apparent discrimination was actually much worse, more than double what it was when dealing with the employers directly. Explicit statements of prejudice against the older candidate were rare, but the employers were four times more likely to say that the older candidate was overqualified. Again the qualifications in fact were identical. Employers were also twice as likely to try to calculate the age of the older candidate than that of the younger.[32] To deal with problems like this, the insurance company Domestic & General Group PLC in the United Kingdom moved its initial job interviews to the telephone to reduce age bias that is more common in face-to-face interviews.[33]

More generally, the evidence that age discrimination happens in employment interviews is overwhelming. A review of twenty-one separate studies of these interviews, including in laboratory settings where other factors can more easily be controlled, finds that biases against older candidates exist that cannot be accounted for by other attributes.[34]

A survey in the IT industry found a majority of employers actually reporting that they would not hire anyone over age forty, exactly the age where candidates are legally protected against age discrimination, which makes these statements blatantly illegal. But the prejudice against older workers in IT is so common that the respondents must have taken for granted that it was acceptable.[35] An additional clue about the problems that older workers face may be found in the length of time IT workers are unemployed. Despite a rather low unemployment rate for IT workers, the duration of unemployment has been rising since 1998. This would be consistent with the view that older IT workers, who are the most likely to be unemployed, have been experiencing a harder time finding new jobs. Among electronic and electrical engineers who were laid off, only 4 percent reported that it was fairly easy to find a new job in the tight labor market of 1998, 76 percent thought that age was an important hindrance to their job search, and older respondents reported significantly more difficulty in their job search.

It would also appear that the perception of IT work and software programming being a young person's game is remarkably common in the industry. The explanations as to why this idea exists, offered by IT employers, include the following:

- Older workers, particularly those with families, cannot or will not work the punishing hours that are typical in software.

- Older workers may not have the skills that are most current. To the extent that the skills are learned in traditional post–secondary education programs, this may be the case, although there are many other ways to learn these skills, and one would think it would be easy to check.

- Older workers may demand more money than younger workers to reward their experience. Yet their additional experience may not be worth much.

- Younger IT managers find it difficult to manage older workers or at least are fearful of trying.[36]

The last point echoes the result of the earlier employer survey.

Conclusion

Some of the consequences of age discrimination are pretty obvious: older candidates do not get hired for positions that they otherwise would, and current employees are dismissed or laid off and passed over for promotions and raises that they otherwise would have received. Discrimination on the job affects current job performance: older individuals who are exposed to negative age stereotypes, for example, perform worse on experimental tests, and their stress levels go up as well.[37] Other consequences extend well beyond employment outcomes. A study of the mental and physical health of seniors found that those who were surrounded by negative stereotypes of aging had worse health outcomes, whereas the reverse was true for those with positive perceptions. The latter group actually lived much longer—7.5 years.[38] Bias against older workers makes them sick.

We now are at the heart of the problem of managing older workers. Despite a compelling business case for retaining and hiring them and despite generally supportive statements from employers about their value, individual hiring managers and supervisors hold negative attitudes toward older workers that are refuted by research. In other words, they are prejudiced. And they make decisions regarding older workers that reflect those negative attitudes.

But the story is not all about negative attitudes on the part of managers. Another part of the problem is revealed in the statistics above about the perception of conflicts between older workers and their typically younger supervisors. In the next chapter, we look at why this is happening and what to do about it.

5

Helping Younger Supervisors

The evidence from earlier chapters indicates that despite a very compelling business case for older workers, we see widespread discrimination against them and a general reluctance to hire them. Much of the concern, and the issue that is hardest to confront with hard research, centers around conflicts that might result when older workers are managed by invariably younger supervisors. As noted earlier, an incredible 88 percent of employer respondents worried about these conflicts, and nearly 60 percent of HR managers at large companies say they've seen significant office conflicts that flow from age-related differences between workers, much of it centered around older subordinates and younger managers.[1] At the heart of the difficulty of getting older workers into successful work relationships, therefore, is the challenge of having younger managers supervise older employees. Why should that be so difficult?

Who's at Fault? Roots of the Conflict

Ninety percent of roughly 260 employers questioned in a recent Society for Human Resource Management survey said they have at least some workers reporting to younger supervisors. Also, close to one-third of those seasoned workers said they have at least a few beefs about it, centering on the boss's lack of real-world experience, according to the survey.[2] The *BusinessWeek* survey cited earlier found 44 percent of executives saying that older workers had difficulty with younger supervisors, and younger workers were likely to think that older subordinates would resist younger supervisors.[3] Whether that is true is an empirical question. A national survey of employees and their workplace arrangements, for example, found that when older workers have younger supervisors, the older subordinates were more likely than their younger counterparts to believe that their supervisor was competent. (One in five of the older workers still have significant problems with their supervisors.)[4]

At least part of the explanation for problems between older subordinates and younger supervisors relates to the simple psychology of attraction: we like people who are similar to us. Other things being equal, we are more comfortable with people who are like us on the attributes we can observe. Older workers prefer to be around older workers, and younger ones prefer to be around younger colleagues. Research shows that the preference for being around people who are similar to us spills over from preferences to workplace outcomes. The more different supervisors are from the subordinates they supervise, other things being equal, the worse the supervisors rate the performance of their supervisees and the more conflict the supervisees see in their work roles and relationships.[5] Younger supervisors may not want to manage older subordinates simply because they are "different" in an important way. Older subordinates similarly may not like to deal with younger supervisors because they are different.

These effects of age similarity are not necessarily big, however, and interestingly, the differences are not always symmetrical. In another study, older supervisors gave higher evaluations to workers in younger work groups, while younger supervisors did the reverse, giving a lower score to those in older work groups.[6] As we saw earlier, the biases are strongly against older workers. In fact, the age group with the greatest preference toward younger people is those of middle age, the age group likely to be mid-level managers.[7] If a simple preference for managing age groups similar to oneself was the issue, it would be difficult to explain the apparent preferences for the more "traditional" model where younger employees were supervised by older managers, as the demographic difference between the two groups would be equally great.

Another and arguably more important part of the explanation for the difficulty in having younger supervisors manage older subordinates turns on our expectations and assumptions about how the workplace operates and what happens when those assumptions are violated. In the traditional workplace, individuals got to be supervisors and higher-level managers through promotions up reasonably clear job ladders. In most cases, explicitly so in unionized contexts, seniority played an important role in determining who got promoted. Managers were older because it took a while to advance up long promotion ladders with many steps. In part they also got promoted because of implicit assumptions that experience was something quite valuable in the next level up. Given this pattern, it was reasonable to expect that supervisors would be older than the people in the lower-level jobs they supervised.

Age Typing

One consequence of these expectations is that they lead to attributions about the individuals in different jobs based on their age, what we might think of as *age typing*. For example, we might assume there is something wrong with workers who are relatively older than their peers in a job hierarchy, that they have been passed over for promotion and therefore are not as good as their younger peers. We might also think there is something wrong, or at least lacking, with managers who are younger than we expect. Perhaps they don't have the level of experience that is truly needed to do the job, or they got their positions through some process that is less than legitimate. In fact, research suggests that employees actually earn less when they are supervised by managers who are younger than the norm; managers earn less when they supervise subordinates whose age is outside the norm as well—either younger or older than is typical.[8] The explanation seems to be that there is some negative signal associated with having employees holding jobs at ages that are "inappropriate."

These assumptions about where in the organization one should be at different ages can lead to problems for the individuals involved. Part of the concern that a manager might have in hiring an older subordinate might reflect the signaling issues above about an older worker's prospects for performance. To paraphrase Groucho Marx, they wouldn't want to hire anyone who would want to work for them: candidates who would be willing to be supervised by a younger manager probably wouldn't be very good. That is certainly a problem, although it is clearly a problem that should be resolved by evidence rather than stereotypes: let's look at the candidates objectively, forgetting their age (which we aren't allowed to ask about in any case), and then decide, are they qualified for the job or not? Even if hired, an older employee whose experience and age should give them more status in their organization but who holds a lower-level job, one populated by younger employees, may well feel that something is wrong with this picture. This inconsistency in their status causes stress, which can lead to unpleasant work-related outcomes.[9]

Special problems come when these expectations cross the supervisor–subordinate boundary, when younger supervisors manage older subordinates. Research evidence indicates that supervisors rate older subordinates lower, other things being equal, again perhaps because of the sense that such subordinates would have been promoted already if they were really good workers.[10] Evidence also suggests that managers tend to explain problems with performance differently for older workers: they are more likely to blame poor performance in older workers on ability or character issues and are less

---

Boomers and Gen Y:
Bookends in the Workplace

Amid the debate on the perceived conflict between younger and older workers, Carolyn Buck Luce from Ernst & Young reminds us that perceptions about age differences are not always reality. She finds that baby boomers and those born between 1982 and 1994 have far more in common than one might think. Both groups want a workplace that is basically the opposite of the traditional white male competitive model. "Both want modular work, meaningful work, and critical experiences; they value leisure time and the role that friends, family, and community play in balancing work," said Buck Luce in a recent interview.[a] The size of these two groups presents a real opportunity and challenge for companies, said Buck Luce: "Companies can either turn their backs on what these employees want, insisting that they work in the traditional white male competitive model, where you come to a place, work seventy hours a week, climb a corporate ladder; or they can get ahead of the curve and use these generational interests to transform the workplace." In essence, the challenge ahead, she said, is to figure out how to redesign work to fit your talent, versus the traditional approach of shoehorning talent to fit the job.

a. Carolyn Buck Luce, telephone interview with Lynn Selhat,.September 9, 2008.

likely to recommend training as a solution than they would for equivalent younger workers.[11] It's the "can't teach old dogs new tricks" stereotype. Interestingly, some of this apparent bias may simply be the result of a lack of experience. Another study finds that we would all likely be happier being managed by older supervisors: they tend to rate otherwise equivalent workers higher and are much more likely to attribute performance problems to issues that are temporary and that can be fixed.[12] Whether the older supervisors are more accurate in their assessments of performance, possibly because of greater experience, or whether they simply have lower expectations about performance is hard to answer. But their greater willingness to fix problems is probably a good thing.

In either case, the negative attributions of younger supervisors about older subordinates create a vicious cycle. They lead to lower performance ratings, and then often to morale problems and conflicts— real performance issues. Younger supervisors expect that they will get less commitment and support from older subordinates, while those older subordinates also expect that they will get less attention from their younger supervisors.[13] These negative attitudes lead to negative attributions. Another study found similar attributions from older employees, that they expected less of younger supervisors and rated them less highly than did younger workers.[14]

Are Differences the Problem?

We saw earlier that the job performance of older workers tends to be better than that of their younger counterparts. But maybe there is something about the way in which they do their jobs that makes it difficult to manage them. One view is that differences in values are the problem. But in a study of three thousand business leaders born between 1925 and 1986 and their life priorities, the values looked quite similar across age groups (see table 5-1).

TABLE 5-1

Top three values, by age group

Silents (b. 1925–1945)	Early boomers (b. 1946–1954)	Late boomers (b. 1955–1963)	Early Xers (b. 1964–1976)	Late Xers (b. 1977–1986)
Family 46%	Family 45%	Family 64%	Family 67%	Family 73%
Integrity 46%	Integrity 32%	Integrity 29%	Love 32%	Love 49%
Love 26%	Love 27%	Love 29%	Integrity 24%	Spirituality 28%
Spirituality 25%	Spirituality 21%	Spirituality 23%	Happiness 20%	Happiness 25%
Self-respect 22%	Self-respect 21%	Happiness 18%	Spirituality 17%	Friendship 25%
Justice 15%	Economic security 15%	Achievement 16%	Self-respect 16%	Self-respect 19%
Wisdom 15%	Competence 14%	Self-respect 14%	Achievement 14%	Help others 13%
Responsibility 10%	Wisdom 13%	Balance 11%	Balance 13%	Integrity 11%
Balance 9%	Happiness 13%	Economic security 10%	Economic security 9%	Economic security 8%
Economic security 9%	Achievement 12%	Wisdom 10%	Friendship 8%	Loyalty 6%

Source: Jennifer Deal, *Retiring the Generation Gap: How Employees Old and Young Can Find Common Ground* (San Francisco: John Wiley & Sons, 2007), 19.

The important differences were not in the actual beliefs or values themselves but more in how people *express* their values. For example, a thank-you note sent by e-mail expresses a similar value as one sent by mail, but different age groups may perceive them quite differently.

A recent study in France looked at the effects of older and younger people working together and debunked many of the standard stereotypes, such as that older people are less willing to take risks.[15] The study also found that the older subjects were generally more cooperative than the younger study subjects. But most important was the finding that cooperation was the highest in groups that had a mix of older and younger people, suggesting that there are great benefits to maintaining an age-diverse workplace.

In addition to values, there may be important differences in the source of motivation by age that affects how people should be managed. Before we turn to see what research suggests about motivational differences by age, it's worth beginning with our own intuition: Imagine yourself in your midsixties. What do you think will be the most important change in how you will view work? For those who are already there, how do you think differently about work now than a generation earlier? For most people, the answers lie with goals, aspirations, and objectives. Our circumstances are so different at these ages that they inevitably spill over to our work and point us to the most basic question: why are we working?

Psychologists Ruth Kanfer and Phillip Ackerman are bringing attention to this question by investigating the differences in motivation between older workers and younger workers.[16] Motivation is not just a "yes/no" factor, whether or not we are willing to do a good job, but something with more complex attributes. The basic question, why do we want to work in the first place, turns out to be of great practical importance for employers because it relates directly to the way in which workplaces are managed, something about which employers have choices. As we will see later in the book, those choices affect their ability to attract and engage older workers, whether they get high levels of performance and value from them.

The most basic age-related differences stem from the fact that people are systematically different in their needs and expectations at different points in their working life. For most of us who begin work right after leaving school, we have relatively few obligations and no prior experiences. We are looking for development, career advancement, and recognition from work; in midcareer, needs shift toward greater interest in money and stability, in part because the earlier needs have at least partially been met and in part because family obligations increase; at the end of our working career, many of these prior needs have been met or at least begin to recede, and we are perhaps more able to focus on different interests.

Laura Carstensen describes this process of changing needs in the context of basic psychological principles. At the beginning of our careers, we are trying to create an identity for ourselves. "Who am I?" is answered in part through our achievements and accomplishments, and our workplace goals center on those accomplishments. Once our identity and sense of our self is established, our focus in later years shifts toward goals that make us feel good about that identity we have already established.[17] Along those lines, there is some evidence that our goals after midlife become more altruistic, including how we might help those around us.[18] More generally, evidence suggests that workplace goals per se become less important as workers age because their interests outside of the workplace push their way forward.[19]

It's not just workplace goals that change. An interesting study suggests that one's tolerance for workplace politics declines for older workers. Office politics in this study were described as self-serving behaviors or "sucking up," as opposed to doing what is in the best interests of the organization. Older workers seem more affected by perceptions of office politics, and it has a negative effect on their job performance. The performance of younger workers was not affected.

Given that they are more focused on individual achievement, perhaps the younger workers are more likely to be the ones driving office politics in the first place.[20]

These age-related differences in motivation, defined broadly, appear to be reinforced by subtle differences in personality that new studies observe over one's life course. Personality refers to one's disposition or tendency to respond in social situations. The consensus had been that personality differences were reasonably stable over time, but more detailed data and investigations now show some consistent changes over time. In absolute terms, the changes are small, but it is interesting nevertheless to see where they point for older workers.

For example, as individuals age, their level of conscientiousness rises. This measures one's sense of duty and is far and away the most important aspect of personality in determining job performance.[21] Agreeableness, the tendency to be compassionate and cooperative, also increases. Such behaviors may be especially important in modern, less structured workplaces and are associated with emotional intelligence. There are slight declines among older workers in neuroticism, the tendency to experience negative emotions such as anger and anxiety in response to situations. All of these suggest that as individuals age, their personalities evolve in ways that make them better employees, or at the very least easier to be around. The only change with any negative aspects for work might be a slight decline in openness (curiosity, imagination, etc.), which has not been found to relate job performance, although one could imagine some jobs where it might be important.[22] Echoing these findings, a recent Dutch study looking at age and personality differences found that older adults were, on average, more agreeable and especially more conscientious than middle-aged and younger adults.[23]

A different study, using measures we might associate with one's mood, shows a similar positive effect with aging. Other things being equal, levels of contentment and enthusiasm tend to rise as we age (see figure 5-1).

FIGURE 5-1

Health and safety needs of older workers

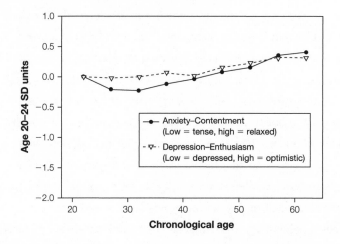

Source: National Research Council, *Health and Safety Needs of Older Workers* (Washington, DC: National Academy Press, 2004).

A Towers Perrin survey of thirty-five thousand employees across large companies in 2003 examined the question of motivation more directly (see "The Motivation Factor") and found that self-reported motivation to do their job was higher for older workers and that the highest levels of motivation were with the oldest cohort of employees, age fifty-five plus.[24] The national study of employees and their workplace arrangements, noted earlier, found that older workers were more satisfied with their jobs and were more likely to express an intention to stay with their employer. And, as noted above, they also thought much more highly of their immediate supervisors than did their younger colleagues, seeing them as not only more competent and more supportive but more responsive to family and personal needs than did younger employees.[25] While it is certainly possible that older employees just have lower expectations than their younger colleagues, it is impossible with these results to see them as complainers or as people who find it hard to be managed by someone younger.

The Motivation Factor

Towers Perrin studied roughly thirty-five thousand employees working for midsize and large U.S. companies and found that employees over age fifty were more motivated to exceed expectations on the job than were younger workers. The same study explored the related concept of *employee engagement,* which Towers Perrin defines as employees' willingness and ability to contribute to company success, or put discretionary effort into their work, in the form of extra time, dedication, and energy. They found that higher levels of engagement correlate with lower turnover, and engaged employees are more likely to work hard to produce high-quality products and services and meet customers' needs. Consequently, the companies that employ them are more likely to exceed the average one-year revenue growth for their industries. No doubt there's a virtuous circle at work here—superior performance enables companies to attract more highly engaged people, and an engaged workforce delivers better performance. What is important is that employee engagement and superior business performance are strongly intertwined.

Source: *The Business Case for Workers Age 50+: Planning for Tomorrow's Talent Needs in Today's Competitive Environment,* report for AARP prepared by Towers Perrin, December 2005, 24, 36.

Or Is the Problem How Younger Supervisors Manage?

The common attributes of older workers, such as their goals and the factors that motivate them, certainly seem to be important, but it is hard to see that those attributes should necessarily cause problems for supervision. So perhaps we should pay more attention to the behavior of their supervisors. There is evidence that they treat older subordinates differently. In one study, younger supervisors with older subordinates were more likely to avoid conflicts and less likely to use collaborative styles of managing conflicts with their older subordinates when problems occurred. Age of the supervisor was the most important factor predicting how supervisors handled conflict.[26]

A second study examined what happened when the structure of the work and how it was organized differed. In the first situation, the supervisors worked more or less side by side with older subordinates as peers. In that context, the older subordinates actually performed better on several dimensions than their younger peers. The second situation was one where the younger supervisors operated more from on high, managing from a separate office. In this case, the older subordinates exhibited behaviors that were associated with dissatisfaction, essentially trying to change their jobs in ways that would give them greater control and influence.[27] What this study suggests is that it might be the apparent status differences that generate problems, not so much the age differences per se.

The Leadership Challenge

We know older workers have different interests and are motivated by different outcomes than are their younger counterparts. We also have some evidence suggesting that the way in which younger supervisors manage their older employees is different from the way they manage other workers and is arguably an especially poor match for the unique attributes of older workers. At the heart of the difficulty in hiring and engaging older workers appears to be this interface with younger supervisors and the approach they take to managing older subordinates.

The business world has been rethinking its ideas about what it means to lead people in organizations for at least a half century (see "The Long Trail of Leadership Reform"). While we might still be a bit fuzzy about what the new view is, the traditional model is very clear.

The Long Trail of Leadership Reform

The notion that the supervisor should have absolute authority based on their superior knowledge was cemented around WWI with the rise of scientific management and the notion that science and engineering in particular could identify the single best way to perform every task. The job of management was to identify that best way; the job of subordinates was to carry it out. Almost immediately, observers began to push back on that notion, first with the human relations school beginning in the 1930s, which recognized that employees had social needs that went beyond the material rewards of the scientific management approach and that managers needed to recognize them. Participative goal setting in the 1950s suggested the importance of having employees involved in determining their own objectives, a notion that extended in the 1970s with the Quality of Work Life Movement and the idea that participation in decision making on all workplace issues was a good thing for improving commitment and performance. The idea that teams could manage themselves, or at least much of their own work, was pushed along by the success of Japanese management approaches,

---

Bosses tell us what to do, and we do it. The reason we do is at least in part that the boss has authority. Some of that authority simply comes from the title and the chain of command inside the organization: the supervisor directs the hourly workers, the manager directs the supervisor, directors boss the managers, and so forth. We accept the organization's rules and the authority structure when we sign on to work there. This formal authority in the hierarchy also gives the supervisors access to information from the leaders about the goals and priorities of the organization. Therefore, they know best about what is going on.

Even more of their authority may come from expertise. Especially in functional areas, such as an accounting or engineering department,

and the idea that leaders might "emerge" from those teamwork settings, rather than be appointed by the organization, followed somewhat naturally. And since then, the notion of empowered employees—where individual workers take the initiative to make decisions themselves—has become a stated goal in most sophisticated organizations. The idea of what it means to be a leader of employees in this context has changed as well. The idea that leadership could be "shared" with subordinates, that leaders should act more like "coaches" than bosses, that managing the social networks rather than the formal bureaucracy was the key objective, all became popular. Despite all these conceptual developments over the decades, the main challenge in leadership, which cuts across all these reform efforts and is especially acute with younger supervisors and older subordinates, remains the basic task of getting leaders to stop acting like the authoritarian engineers of WWI and involve their subordinates in decisions. For a good review of the history of reforms, see C. Pearce, and J. A. Conger, "All Those Years Ago: The Historical Underpinnings of Shared Leadership," in *Shared Leadership: Reframing the Hows and Whys of Leadership,* eds. C. Pearce and J. A. Conger (New York: Wiley, 2003), 1–18.

---

we assume the boss knows more about the function than we do because he or she has done our job before, apparently performing it well enough to be promoted, and has seen more of the problems in this area than we have. Some of that authority comes from more general experience, where bosses have seen a lot of developments in our business or industry. Because the bosses have had more experience, we would expect them to be older than the people they supervise.

Younger supervisors have a big problem in trying to lead or manage with this model of authority. The obvious reason is that older subordinates, other things being equal, have more experience than the younger managers. Older workers often have deeper functional expertise and have certainly seen more, sometimes in the context of the current company or at least in the same industry or business. Where they have worked elsewhere, they may have broader knowledge about the different ways that tasks can be performed and work organized. In some cases, they have held senior positions elsewhere and therefore know quite a bit about how senior executives think. How can a younger supervisor compete with this?

The answer is, they can't. A supervisor who expects to manage or lead based on authority has a big problem with older, more experienced subordinates. We can now see why, especially, a less experienced, insecure supervisor would be reluctant to hire older and more experienced subordinates, even if that view was not something they would articulate explicitly, because that experience undermines their own authority. This situation might well explain much of the negative attributions directed at older workers, the ones that research refutes, such as their performance is worse or their ability to get along with people is not so good. It is difficult for a younger supervisor to articulate their real concern, which is that they are afraid to hire someone more experienced than they are. So instead, they rationalize their resistance to hire them with these other attributions about older workers.

The archetype of the conflict of experience occurs in the military, where young, junior officers, typically just out of the military academies or ROTC programs, are sent to lead experienced personnel. We've probably all seen the movie version of what happens next: the tough and experienced troops laugh behind the back of the wet-behind-the-ears lieutenant, who makes one mistake after another before the older sergeant steps in and straightens things out.

Lessons from the Military

Jerry David, an air force chief master sergeant and a forty-year veteran, experienced two generations of junior officers stepping into this situation. "In the old days, the young officers would come in like a bull in a china shop, trying to prove how much they knew and trying to assert their authority. That's how a lot of them got killed in Vietnam, by not listening to the older and much more experienced troops," David says. Over time, the military began to recognize the problem. "Now the senior leadership drums it into the heads of the junior officers that they don't know anything yet and that they need to start building relationships with the enlisted men."[28]

Business author, Wharton alumnus, and former Marine Corps artillery officer Jason Santamaria explains that his single most important leadership lessons came when he was one of those twenty-six-year-old lieutenants commanding a first sergeant almost twice his age. After his first day, the sergeant told him, "Sir, your plan failed because you did not consult the experienced leaders in this unit." In other words, him. (Or as Jerry David told a young lieutenant, "Sir, you can do anything you want. Just ask me first.") Officers in the Marines are now trained in leaderless teams, where the group has to work together to solve complex tasks without any formal authority structure. Once given a commission, young lieutenants are placed in formal "leadership partnerships" with older and experienced sergeants. Despite the fact that the lieutenant outranks the sergeant, they are expected to work as a team and to learn from each other.[29]

The military academies also address the challenge of having junior officers lead older and more experienced personnel. West Point rotates majors and captains from command positions back into the academy to offer practical guidance to cadets on the challenges of leading in the field, and the issue of working with older noncommissioned officers features prominently in those discussions. The Naval Academy takes a more structured, classroom-based approach to the topic through its required leadership courses. Donald Horner, a leadership professor there, describes the underlying model as beginning with an understanding of the attributes of the officer and of the personnel they command: how do differences or similarities in age between us affect the approach I should take to lead each group?

Age Difference Doesn't Matter

Jason McCormick and Bill Sheikewitz have a fairly typical employment relationship. McCormick, director of the race and sports book at Red Rock Resort, supervises Sheikewitz's activities as a race and sports ticket writer. McCormick sets betting lines, monitors incoming wagers, and helps set Sheikewitz's and other ticket writers' work schedules.

There's just one peculiarity between the two: At sixty-one, Sheikewitz is old enough to be his thirty-one-year-old *supervisor's* father. He retired from a forty-year career with the New York Stock Exchange, where he ultimately ended up as director of floor operations. Four years ago, he moved to Las Vegas to pursue his "fantasy job" of working in a race and sports book. After writing tickets at a smaller casino, Sheikewitz joined Red Rock when it opened in April. He sees having a young boss as a natural part of his second career.

"The age difference isn't a factor," Sheikewitz said. "If the manager you work under leads by example, keeps a constructive relationship with you, and treats you with respect, age doesn't matter. Jason listens. He leads by example. He keeps constructive relationships. He's extremely approachable and he's honest."

"You need to offer respect in return," said McCormick, who estimated that about 200 of the 250 people who report to him are older than he is. "If I have respect for them and what they want to accomplish on the job and in life, that respect is returned to me."

Source: Jennifer Robison, "Youth Served, by Elders," *Las Vegas Review-Journal*, Mar 5, 2007.

Lessons from Singapore

An interesting attempt to address these supervisor–subordinate conflicts comes from Singapore, where the need to get older individuals into the workforce is especially acute. Average life expectancy in

Singapore increased from sixty-one years around 1960 to eighty at present, blowing well past the traditional retirement age of sixty-two. Before the 2009 financial crisis, unemployment rates hovered between 2 and 3 percent, and labor shortages were a challenge for companies. There was a real need both for the older individuals and for the employers to expand job opportunities.

At the same time, age-related conflicts are particularly acute in Asian countries like Singapore because of the respect traditionally given to older individuals. The idea that a young person might boss around an elder was anathema in that culture. Bringing older workers back into jobs with younger bosses created big conflicts: the younger managers in many cases resisted even trying to manage their older subordinates, and the latter were often embarrassed to ask when they needed help, and resisted taking direction when it was offered.

Before an employer in Singapore embarks on a program to bring in more older workers, they are offered a tripartite (government-employer-union) training program to prepare all parties for the new arrangement. Catherine Choo, who leads some of those training engagements, explains that the underlying problems in these situations are rooted in a lack of understanding, trust, and respect. The biggest mistake that the younger supervisors make is to avoid conflict by avoiding the older subordinate, leaving them to work independently without guidance.

The training program they offer teaches both sides—younger supervisors and older subordinates—first about themselves, to be aware of their own biases, personality, and ways of interacting. Then it teaches communication skills and, for the supervisors, coaching skills. Choo offers these lessons for supervisors:

1. Spend time to build relationships with the senior staff.

2. Create a work culture that encourages mutual respect—you respect their experience and expertise, they respect the role you play in directing the employer's goals.

3. Lead by example rather than formal authority.

4. Experiment to find the most effective ways to relate to and coach the older staff.

Singapore also promotes an important innovation for workers who are continuing past the usual retirement age with their employer: an explicit recontracting of the relationship. The employee sits down with the management team and draws up what the job will look like going forward, how it will differ from what the employee did before in tasks, performance standards, and rates of pay. The important point behind this exercise is to manage the expectations of all parties.

Harvey Sterns, director of the Institute for Life-Span Development and Gerontology at the University of Akron, notes the risk that sensitivity training for organizations about older workers—that drawing attention to stereotypes of any kind—can cause individuals to focus on them and actually pay more attention to them. Sterns echoes the lesson from the Singapore approach that older workers themselves have important work to do in adjusting their own expectations; it can't all be done by the organization or by younger supervisors. For example, he notes that the declining tolerance for organizational politics that is common among older workers can easily be seen as intolerance and grumpiness. "Curmudgeons," he observes, "are good in literature but hard to live with."[30]

Conclusion

Much of the difficulty that older workers have in getting hired and then functioning successfully in the workplace appears to center on the relationship with younger supervisors, at the point of hiring and then later when work is being done. The heart of that problem centers on leadership styles that are a particularly poor fit with older workers, an authority-driven approach to supervision. It obviously takes two to have a conflict, so why focus so much attention on the younger supervisor? One reason is that they are the ones initiating and defining the relationship. Even in participatory models of management, they ought to be the ones shaping the terms of the relationship. But we shouldn't let the older workers off the hook, either. A useful lesson from the Singapore experience is the effort to influence attitudes and behavior on both sides, to shape the expectations of the older workers as well before the relationship with the younger supervisor even begins.

6

Crafting a Better Deal for Older Workers

Earlier chapters outlined the business case for hiring older workers and described the key challenge of getting younger supervisors to manage differently, in a more participative manner. But while the relationship with supervisors may be the key issue, it is not the whole story about how to make use of the older workforce. What else should employers do to best engage older workers?

A Mismatch with the Corporate Model

A good place to start is with a reminder that older employees probably have more interests in common with their younger counterparts than they have differences. Everyone wants to be treated with respect; everyone wants attractive working conditions, good wages and benefits, and interesting work. An employer that struggles with attracting, retaining, and motivating their average employees will no doubt find the same challenge with older workers. Similarly, many of the "best practices" for managing older workers are good practices for all employees. In fact, one of the main lessons from this book is that employers don't have to turn their organization on its head to succeed with older workers.

With that in mind, we can concentrate on the points of difference between older workers and their younger counterparts in the workplace, the attributes that are especially important for older individuals. The obvious place to begin thinking about how to craft a set of practices and policies that are attractive to older workers is with the fact that they are coming to the end of their careers. Many of the most important techniques that U.S. businesses in particular use to motivate and manage their employees are in fact targeted at those who are in the early and middle stages of their careers, and are based on the fading notion of lifetime careers. The most important of these are promotion opportunities. Historically, U.S. corporations relied on the promise of promotions as the main instrument for motivating employees, especially white-collar workers. With promotions came greater prestige, greater influence, and greater money.

It is hard to imagine anything less interesting to most older workers than the opportunity to compete for promotions. Those who have had career success already have experienced the joys and headaches of leadership positions at the top of hierarchies. Those who have had less career success are unlikely to be motivated by the possibility of promotions now, at the end of their careers, having either shifted their priorities to other goals or rationalized their different path. Nor do they have the time left in their careers for the prospect of an eventual promotion to be attractive. As the studies cited earlier indicate, the type of competition and the office politics associated with the competition for promotions are the workplace attributes viewed most negatively by older workers.

A second mismatch with older workers is the focus on financial rewards. While it is certainly true that money is of interest to older workers, it is also of substantially less interest to most of them than to their younger colleagues, who still face the most significant of life's financial challenges: buying houses, college tuition for children, and saving for retirement. The promise of big bonuses and potentially big payoffs, especially in the long run, is not irrelevant to older workers, but it is clearly of less interest to those whose biggest financial challenges are more likely to be behind them.

The third and perhaps worst mismatch with older workers is to rely on the fear of being fired as the means to motivate and manage employees. Few employers are so negative in their orientation as to literally threaten employees with dismissals to keep them in line, although individual supervisors may be less circumspect. But many employers effectively fall back on the fear of being fired as the default management technique because they don't offer much else to motivate and manage their workforce. To keep the employees performing, they rely on knowing that their employees can't afford to lose their jobs. While nobody wants to be fired, older workers may well find this less terrifying—they may not expect to work much longer in any case, they may not need the money, work may be less central to their lives, and so forth.

There is a big mismatch, therefore, between the way some employers and supervisors deal with their employees and the interests and needs of older workers. Relying on money, on promotions, on threats of job loss—extrinsic rewards—for motivation is unlikely to be very effective. As noted earlier, relying on formal and expert authority for supervision also has low prospects for success and is often part of an approach that focuses on extrinsic rewards. (The reason is that with the boss making most of the decisions, employees are not likely to find the work very satisfying, and the only thing they may get out of it is money.) It could well be that some of the resistance to hiring older workers is based at least implicitly on a recognition by employers that the models of management they use are less likely to be effective with older workers.

A study of older workers across the European Union found other common mismatches in the management of older workers, especially where the way work was organized created unnecessarily boring jobs. Specifically:

- Older workers were less likely to be working in teams and more likely to be on tasks by themselves, isolating them socially at a point in their lives where one of their greatest needs is for social interaction.

- Their jobs offered fewer opportunities to solve novel problems or to learn new skills, leading to boring work.

- Older workers were disproportionately kept on independent tasks and away from teams, making it difficult to learn from others and leading to further isolation.

- Their tasks made less use of computers and the Internet, proxies for more challenging work.

- Finally, they were less likely to receive training, to be taking education courses, or to be involved in activities associated with lifelong learning.[1]

It is almost as if older workers were an asset that employers were getting ready to use up and dispose of, keeping them on the same job to squeeze out returns from long-ago investments. Without opportunities to learn new skills or improve their existing ones, older workers were guaranteed to become obsolete. Isolated and boring jobs almost ensured that they would burn out. These conclusions matched those of a survey of older U.S. workers who report their perception that employers see their value as being limited to their current role. This creates a vicious circle: employers don't invest in their skills or provide opportunities for them to learn new ones, so they are indeed limited in their ability to contribute beyond their current role.[2]

What "Deal" Do Older Workers Want?

The place to begin thinking about how to manage the older worker is how to get them in the door. Many don't have to work for pay, in some cases especially the employees who employers really need: those with highly specialized skills and knowledge who have been well compensated in the past. Bringing retirees back into the same organization raises a special challenge, as those workers have already decided once to leave. Offering them the same arrangements they had before is unlikely to be the best way to get them to come back.

A RetirementJobs.com survey of job seekers over age fifty reports their priorities in assessing the attractiveness of potential jobs: flexibility (69 percent rated it important); security and stability (67 percent); independence and autonomy (65 percent); service and dedication (58 percent); cash compensation (53 percent); benefits (48 percent); and pure challenge (46 percent).[3] The results hold up even for individuals who have had lower income: it isn't just the well-off who value items other than money highly. Two focus groups conducted by Boston College's Center on Aging and Work—one with low- and middle-income individuals forty years and older seeking retraining for work, and one with middle- and upper-income older workers thinking about career planning— reiterated many of these themes. When asked what they were looking for in work, these individuals focused on making a contribution, keeping social connections, and being able to use their skills and experience. Even in the low-income group, income and health benefits were mentioned only occasionally in the conversation.[4]

AARP's research has also shown older workers' strong preferences for jobs that meet social needs. In two recent national surveys that asked workers age forty-five to seventy what they wanted from work, more than half of working retirees and those about to hit traditional retirement age said it's very important to work where:

- Employee opinions are valued.

- They can work as long as they want to.

- They can take time off to care for relatives.

- They can set their own hours.[5]

While all workers might find these attributes attractive, they were the top priorities for these older workers. Money and opportunities for promotion didn't make the list. These priorities align with what HR and benefits managers told us about engaging older workers, who note that instead of fretting about salaries, the employer should be asking questions like "How can we make our employees' lives easier?" "What can we do to relieve stress and allow for better work-life balance?" "How can we show our employees that we value them, their skills and experience?" Because these attributes are important to all workers—just more so for older ones—pursuing them puts the focus on being a great place to work for everyone. As Kathy Gubanich from Vanguard told us, "You want to introduce programs that appeal to everyone, even if they appeal for different reasons."[6] Again, this doesn't require standing the organization on its head to make it attractive to older workers. But the big advantage of meeting these needs for older workers is that they are likely to lead to an even bigger payoff, a bigger effect on recruiting and retaining engaged older workers at a lower cost in terms of wages and other aspects of compensation.

Even more useful than asking what older workers want is to see what they actually do. When they take new positions, what do they entail? A recent study followed up with employees age fifty-one to fifty-five ten years after starting a new job and found that about half who left their employer moved on to a new one, and of those,

Taking Cues from Working Women

Companies looking for a starting point in dealing with their aging workforces can learn something by looking at policies designed to retain highly skilled women, where a great deal of effort has already been under way. Ernst & Young, in collaboration with the Center for Work-Life Policy, began looking at what they call the "hidden brain drain" several years ago in response to concerns that highly educated women were leaving the workforce in droves.[a] Among highly qualified professionals, women were far more likely to "opt out" of the workforce. Women's reasons for wanting to return to work are strikingly similar to why older people want to work. While money tended to be more important for this younger group than for mature workers, 43 percent cited enjoyment from their work and 24 percent reported cited a desire to give back as important motivations. The remedies for bringing them back are appropriate for older workers as well: reduced-hour jobs, schedule flexibility, staying in touch with employees who have left, and offering opportunities for professional growth, especially to make up for knowledge gaps created during time off.

a. Sylvia Ann Hewlett and Carolyn Buck Luce, "Off-Ramps and On-Ramps: Keeping Talented Women on the Road to Success," *Harvard Business Review*, March 2005, 43–54.

two-thirds moved into a new occupation. On average, they moved into jobs that paid less—57 percent less—and were lower in prestige. A common move was out of management positions into less stressful roles outside of management. And here's the point: they report liking their new jobs better than their old ones. They were happy to trade lower pay and prestige at this point in their career for less stress.[7] (See "Taking Cues from Working Women" for other points that may be pertinent to older workers' job satisfaction.)

Becoming an Employer of Choice for Mature Workers

Lead with the Mission

As we saw from the survey data in chapter 1, one of the more distinctive issues for older workers is the extent to which they are motivated by the chance to contribute something, by wanting to be useful. Those needs point to the importance of a sense of mission as part of the value proposition for attracting older workers. There are two parts to that sense of mission. The first is the importance of doing good, of contributing something important to the community and to others (see "Means and Meaning"). For workers to achieve that goal, a key factor is, who is the recipient or beneficiary of the work? Even though the tasks may be identical—say, a cost accounting project—most people feel differently about it if the client is a community-based nonprofit, as opposed to a for-profit corporation. The issue for an employer that wants to attract older workers is to highlight the social purposes that their organization serves, perhaps even assigning older workers to those projects that target community interests and good works. Most large employers are engaged in projects explicitly targeted to benefit the broader community. We know that many older workers actively volunteer—at no pay—to work on similar projects elsewhere, so companies ought to be able to tap into that workforce without having to pay a lot.

A second, more general aspect of mission gets at the more basic sense of being useful, of making a contribution, that was highlighted in chapter 1's surveys. Here the issue is less the overall goal of the organization and the ultimate recipient of its services and more the way in which individuals perform their tasks. In this case, a key factor is the extent to which individuals can see the connection between what they are doing in their individual job and the overall service or product being produced. The sense of making a contribution can also be enhanced through explicit recognition of an individual's

Means and Meaning

In the 1960s, when President Kennedy famously asked young people to think about what they could do for their country instead of the other way around, he set the tone for a new kind of civic engagement. Today, those same young people are now entering their sixties and once again asking what they can do for their country. As a result, many baby boomers are looking for careers that combine money, meaning, and social impact. Marc Freedman, founder of the nonprofit organization Civic Ventures, calls these *encore careers*. Civic Ventures recently joined with the MetLife Foundation to quantify the extent of encore careers in America:[a]

- A large number of people between the ages of forty-four and seventy—a total of 5.3 million to 8.4 million people, or 6 to 9.5 percent of this population—have already launched encore careers.

- A majority of Americans age forty-four to seventy want meaningful work. More than half of those already in encore careers (55 percent) and two-thirds of people interested in encore careers (64 percent) say they are motivated by a desire to use their skills and experience to help others.

- Eighty-four percent of those in encore careers say they get either a "tremendous amount of satisfaction" (38 percent) or "quite a bit of satisfaction" (46 percent) from their encore careers.

- Most of those in encore careers come from professional and white-collar jobs (88 percent), have at least a college education (67 percent), and tend to live in cities and their surrounding suburbs (72 percent).

a. See *MetLife Foundation/Civic Ventures Encore Career Survey,* http://civicventures.org/surveys.cfm.

performance, highlighting and reinforcing what an individual has contributed to projects or to joint efforts. It is also possible to enhance the sense of mission even in jobs that are otherwise rather pedestrian. Lyndon Johnson often told a story about visiting NASA's Cape Kennedy during the Apollo space program and asking a truck driver what he did there. The driver replied, "I'm helping to put a man on the moon." Psychologists who study the workplace call this concept *task significance*, helping individuals see how their individual tasks contribute to the overall goal of the organization. In virtually every case, that overall mission and goal is much more satisfying and motivating than the individual task one is performing. Enhancing task significance in this manner not only builds motivation, it also helps individuals see how their work fits into the work of others in the organization, enhancing quality efforts.

Other aspects of the way jobs are performed also help meet those intrinsic needs associated with feeling good about one's job. An important one especially for older workers who have expertise and experience is working on a task over which they have some control, so that when it is finished, it is possible to look at it and say, "I did that." The importance of a sense of autonomy in how one performs tasks is well known in research on job satisfaction and seems to be even more important for older workers.[8]

Social Relationships

Another attribute of work that is particularly important for older workers is the ability to develop and maintain relationships with others (see "Social Software Keeps Retirees Connected to the Company"). Interestingly, this is also a top-rated concern for college graduates just entering the workforce. Many of L.L.Bean's employees, both at its flagship store in Freeport, Maine, and in its call centers, are retirees who work because they enjoy having contact with people. L.L.Bean's older employees, when polled by the HR team, say that a sense of camaraderie is one of the main reasons for staying with the company. Their wish for social relationships, along with a desire for flexibility, are a perfect match for L.L.Bean's business model, which has a fairly predictable sales cycle and one big season (Christmas) per year. L.L.Bean's reputation for outstanding customer service is in part due to its older employees, says Kim Fillipone, in L.L.Bean's HR department. To promote camaraderie and help employees interact with each other, L.L.Bean's offices are open and casual, and the company hosts barbeques for all of its employees, including those who work part-time or sporadically.

GlaxoSmithKline tackles the challenge of building social relationships and support systems for older employees at work with a tried-and-true approach used for women and minority employees: creating an "affinity group" at the workplace. Its Prime Time Partners Network, started in 2007, is targeted at mid- and later-career employees, bringing them together at lunch-hour meetings and other occasions with programs on "life phase transitions" that focus on the interests of older workers and retirees who have come back for part-time and project work, such as retirement planning and health and wellness for older individuals. Like other affinity groups at the company, this one is supported by a senior executive sponsor but led by the employees themselves. And the not-so-hidden agenda behind programs like these is for employees to meet and network with other people in similar situations, helping to create systems of support.[9]

Flexibility and Work-Life Balance

The discussion of employee needs earlier pointed to the importance of flexible schedules in attracting and engaging mature workers, in part because work is less likely to be the focus of their lives. A 2002 Conference Board survey of 150 senior human resource managers produced a list of offerings companies are using to retain older workers, as shown in table 6-1.

Social Software Keeps Retirees
Connected to the Company

Anyone with teenagers knows about the popularity of social networks like MySpace and Facebook. These kinds of Web sites, which appeal to youngsters' thirst for immediate communication and information sharing, are now finding their way into corporate America.

Anne Berkowitch, CEO of SelectMinds, a provider of corporate social networking solutions, says that many companies are using these kinds of networks to stay in touch with retirees. "Our clients are Global 2,000 companies, generally large professional services companies. These companies are looking at losing 40 percent to 50 percent of their senior management in the next five years," she says. "These are people who possess a great deal of judgment and experience, who know how to get things done in a company, and know how to build and leverage relationships."[a] Berkowitch says that some of the companies use the networks first to stay in touch with retirees and then to bring them back for part- or full-time positions, for consulting, serving as mentors, leading training sessions, and so forth.

Dow Chemical, one of SelectMinds' clients, deployed a social networking platform in 2007 to address some of the knowledge management problems associated with its aging and soon-to-retire workforce (40 percent of Dow's global workforce will be eligible to retire through 2013) as well as a general shortage of engineering talent.

With forty thousand retirees in the United States alone, Dow had already taken small steps toward staying in touch with retirees, such as through newsletters. But the social networking site offers greater dynamism and opportunities for information exchange. Users who log on to the network are encouraged to use the site as a resource to reconnect with colleagues (retirees can find and connect with each other as well as with current and former employees), expand their professional networks, share news about themselves, or search job opportunities.[b]

Just three months after Dow launched the site, there were more than forty-five hundred network members, and users had applied for twenty-four full-time jobs and forty contract jobs at Dow.[c]

a. Anne Bercowitch, interview with Lynn Selhat, 2007.

b. Thomas Otter and Nikos Drakos, "Case Study: Dow's Formula for Social Software," Gartner RAS Core Research Note G00156018, March 27, 2008.

c. Ibid.

At the top of the list is flexible schedules, and more than half of the total items relate to reductions or changes in working time. Flexibility in terms of work schedules is crucial to other employees as well as it is the key tool for addressing work-life balance issues (see "Be Flexible or Lose Out"). Much of the need for better balance in the workplace for all employees comes from family demands, which

TABLE 6-1

Incentives offered by employers to help retain older workers

Flexible work arrangements	41%
Training to upgrade skills	34%
Time off for volunteerism	15%
Phased retirement	14%
Reduced shift-work	14%
Job rotation	12%
Sabbaticals	11%
Reduced responsibility	8%
Mentoring as a primary job responsibility	5%

Source: *Valuing Experience: How to Motivate and Retain Mature Workers*, based on a 2002 survey of 150 senior human resource executives, The Conference Board, 2003.

Be Flexible or Lose Out

Alison Thurau, system director, human resources, Lee Memorial Health System in Cape Coral, Florida, may have one of the toughest jobs around: staffing a health system that includes five hospitals and numerous outpatient health-care centers. Facing a full-scale nursing shortage, Thurau and her team continually review their HR and benefits offerings to ensure they are able to attract and retain the best employees. "People want to work longer; they just don't want to work the same hours as they did when they were younger," says Thurau.[a] Lee offers numerous scheduling options, including flexible scheduling, which allows employees to determine the number of shifts they work, as well as the number of hours in each shift; job sharing, where two people can split a job; and seasonal months off, where employees can take up to one year off without losing their job or their benefits. "In the seasonal time-off program, we see mainly people taking the summer months off," says Thurau. Of the fifty-six people currently opting for this plan, the majority are fifty and older. According to Thurau, breaking out of the traditional "shift work" mentality requires a great deal of flexibility and creativity. "Flexible scheduling gives us a big advantage when it comes to recruiting and retaining employees," she says.

a. Alison Thurau, telephone interview by Lynn Selhat, August 13, 2008.

are highly unpredictable as they are often driven by problems like health issues. What we know from research is that giving employees some control over their schedules, not just flexibility per se, has a big effect on reducing the stress they feel at work.

Flexible work arrangements come in a variety of configurations, but at the core are these four elements:

- *When to work.* This includes flextime, in which employees have flexible start and stop times or take time off during the day but still work a regular thirty-five-to-forty-hour workweek. (Some companies require all employees to be at work during certain core hours.) Other options are compressed workweeks, where for example instead of working five days a week, employees work four ten-hour days; part-time work, which could mean reduced weekly or annual hours; and seasonal work—that is, clocking in just six months of the year, such as during the busy winter season in Florida. Still more flexible work arrangements include summers off, weekends only, or even three months on, three months off.

- *Where to work.* Options include telecommuting, or working from home either all week or part of the week; or working in more than one location if an employer has more than one office or branch.

- *How to work.* This might be job sharing, which means splitting one job between two employees, with salary and benefits prorated; phased retirement or cutting back on hours over a period of time before fully retiring, often continuing to receive pension or health-care benefits; or temporary, contract, or even per diem work.

- *What to receive for working.* This involves choosing specific benefits—whether for child care or elder care, for instance— or a flexible spending account. Benefits depend on an employee's needs and stage of life.[10]

The most common of these arrangements are flextime and telecommuting. But these are not either-or choices. Some employees, for example, can put together part-time or temporary jobs at more than one workplace to achieve better balance.

Not surprisingly, employers are willing to provide the greatest flexibility for those employees who are the most valuable. Employees who do unstructured tasks are the easiest to offer flexibility to because their work is already somewhat uncoupled from that of the people around them. For example, Deloitte Consulting developed a Senior Leaders Program in 2000 specifically for star executives over fifty. Given that these are highly paid consultants whose pensions vest at fifty, this group is at risk of walking out the door and taking all of their accumulated knowledge and contacts with them. The program basically allows the leaders to write their own tickets: they decide where they want to work, whether they want to work full- or part-time, whether they want to change job functions, and so forth. The program works because these senior leaders know the projects that are important for them and for the firm, and now they have earned the chance to pursue them. They have demonstrated their good judgment over a long career. While the firm approves these work arrangements, it isn't taking much of a risk by letting these leaders define their own assignments.

Similarly, Draper Labs offers extreme job flexibility to retain older workers. Its scientists can take six months off a year, or work an eight-hour day just three days a week, or come up with whatever schedule meets their needs.[11] And employers like Kaye/Bassman International Corporation offer telecommuting to mature staff to keep them from retiring.[12] One of the most novel examples of flexible work takes place at CVS, as it involves seasonal changes in location. As retirees head to Florida every winter, the demand for pharmacy services there grows considerably. CVS Pharmacy's "snowbirding" program provides a neat solution. It has pharmacies in the north and in Florida, and many of its retirees as well as part-time mature workers also head to Florida in the winter—or want to if they had the money. So CVS offers them winter jobs in Florida, where many were headed anyway, saving the cost of putting together a new, seasonal workforce there every year. When the weather improves and they are ready to head back north, that's also when demand falls off in Florida. So when the retirees go back north, the jobs simply end.[13]

Training to Upgrade Skills

The number two incentive for older workers on the Conference Board survey (see table 6-1) is to offer opportunities for older workers to upgrade their skills. More generally, as noted in chapter 3, the chance to learn new things was one of the top reasons why older individuals say they want to keep working. Training may be especially important for older workers whose self-confidence in changing jobs or roles can be low.

The problem for employers is that training can be expensive—not just the training per se, but the most important part of training expenditures tends to be the costs of paying the employees while they learn. Employers might have a special reluctance to pay for the training of individuals who won't stay around long enough to allow the employer to recoup the costs of the training. While the evidence presented earlier suggests that older workers have significantly lower rates of turnover than their younger counterparts, it is fair to say that mature workers who are coming back into work or coming to a new employer at the end of their careers may not stay that long. So what should an employer do in this situation?

A reasonable solution is to create arrangements where the employees can share the costs of the training. The Fair Labor Standards Act requires that employers pay not only for the training costs but also for the time spent in training for hourly employees, which prohibits cost sharing, at least for those employees covered by the act. An increasingly common alternative is to provide opportunities for getting skills up-to-date before candidates become employees. A typical approach is to direct potential applicants to community college course work or other educational providers that offer vocational skills. Sometimes the classes are designed specifically to prepare students for particular employers and jobs. And the evidence suggests that many of the students in community colleges are there to pick up job skills: 28 percent of community college students taking nondegree courses already have a bachelor's degree or higher, and the courses they take tend to be vocational.[14] Some employers require that applicants complete courses at community college as a condition for applying for a position. In these situations, the applicants are paying for the training in advance, although sometimes the employer subsidizes the programs to make it possible for more people to participate in them.

Other arrangements allow employees to take training once they are employed, but on their own time. The big temporary-help agencies, for example, offer modular classes on computer and office skills that the agency employees can take on their own time when they are not otherwise on assignment. The agency benefits from these skills by being able to place the employees in higher-skill, higher-paying jobs, and the employees benefit from better placements.

Companies like Adecco offer a range of in-house classroom training, online training, and certification classes.[15] The Adecco temps can take these training programs whenever they want—entirely voluntarily—and do so on their own time, basically investing in themselves. The advantage for the agency from this is that if the temps improve their skills, they can be placed in higher-paying assignments, which generates more revenue. Adecco has introduced specific types of training with older workers in mind through its Renaissance Program, which promotes mature workers to employers. These clinics include résumé-writing skills, computer literacy skills, and so forth.

Another popular arrangement for sharing costs is tuition assistance or reimbursement programs. Under these arrangements, the employer pays the cost of attending classes, but the employees typically attend them and do the homework on their own time, without pay. Ultimately, the employee ends up making the bigger investment. The employers still have to recoup the investment in tuition, and they do so in part by attracting higher-quality applicants. It's easy to see how this would happen. Any employee who is willing to go to school in the evenings and on weekends while working full-time is a hard worker, and those individuals are the ones attracted to employers that offer tuition assistance. How much more productive or effective would a worker have to be to pay off the costs of using tuition assistance? About 10 percent better for the average worker *in just one year* is enough to recoup the employer's costs for the typical worker who makes use of the program, less for higher-value employees. If the employee's performance is even trivially above average for more than one year, the employer makes money on the investment. Or putting it differently, a very small increment in productivity advantage over the several years an employee is likely to be with the organization makes it worthwhile.

Hospital systems, facing growing shortages of nurses, have been particularly advanced in bringing education to their employees. Lee Memorial Hospital, for example, offers full- and part-time employees working at least sixteen hours per week tuition reimbursement, in-house classroom training, online training, certification classes, nurse refresher programs, and graduate nurse internships.[16] A Lee spokesperson says that career development and maintaining and enhancing skills are a priority for them. The program has also helped in recruiting and retaining talent. Scripps in San Diego provides similar programs, having partnered with community colleges to bring education to the workplace. These programs are available to employees of all ages, but they are particularly helpful at attracting and retaining experienced workers. For example, nurses reentering the workforce after having raised their children find that their skills need to be updated, but the prospect of going back to work and school at the same time can be daunting. On-site classes offer these experienced nurses with highly coveted skills a level of flexibility they need to reenter the workforce.

The second surprising finding is that these programs are associated with lower rates of turnover.[17] Perhaps the employees are

New York City Teaching Fellows

To recruit teachers, the New York City Teaching Fellows program offers older workers experienced in other fields a seven-week training program. This program essentially converts individuals who have had no prior experience into teachers, offering the opportunity to switch careers, something many people (but especially older employees) like. And the mission of teaching, especially in urban environments, is especially attractive to many older individuals. Once the new teaching fellows begin teaching, the program offers them support, through tuition reimbursement programs, to complete their teaching education by earning a master's degree.[a] This program is effectively a trifecta of opportunities for older workers: offering them the opportunity to pursue a job with a strong mission, to change careers, and to upgrade skills and keep learning in the process.

a. Toddi Gutner, "Still Working and Loving It," *BusinessWeek*, February 15, 2006, http://www.businessweek.com/magazine/content/06_42/b4005101.htm.

simply staying around to complete their education, but even so, it takes many years to do that, and on average, those who use the programs stay longer.

Benefits

Good benefits, like good wages, are important to almost all workers. But because older workers have some different interests from their younger counterparts, they also find particular sets of benefits attractive. And some employers have targeted those benefits in an effort to attract older workers. To illustrate:

- Bon Secours Richmond Health System offers college scholarships for employees' children and grandchildren.[18] The children of many older workers are already too old to make use of scholarships and tuition assistance aimed at children, so a program that offers benefits to grandchildren is obviously important for these older workers.

- St. Mary's Medical Center allows retirees to purchase medication at cost.[19]

- Lee Memorial sponsors the Senior Health Activities Resource Education Club for older workers and retirees. It offers health screenings, claims filing assistance, discount prescriptions, and retirement planning education.[20]

- Anheuser-Busch Adventure Parks offers long-term-care coverage for employees, their parents, and their grandparents. Although employees of any age can make use of this benefit, it may be especially important and desirable for those who think they may need it themselves or for their spouses.

- United Technologies Corporation's Employee Scholar Program offers educational opportunities for older workers to attain college degrees and to keep learning. Its program goes well beyond a simple tuition reimbursement program in that it allows employees to pursue course work in any field, whether or not the education is useful at work. It also rewards participants with stock grants for completing degree programs.[21]

Specific Tools for Attracting Mature Workers

Going to the labor market with an attractive value proposition is a great way to begin, but employers interested in targeting mature workers will have to do some active recruiting as well.

Employers that may not have the marketing resources to target older workers themselves are increasingly using specialized agencies. Summit Machine, for example, had difficulty recruiting young employees for manufacturing work and turned to Mature Staffing to recruit experienced technicians, who, they found, turned out to be more effective than their younger counterparts.[22] Mature Staffing is one of a growing number of online job boards that cater to older workers. Some are for-profit and others are run by nonprofit organizations. In particular, AARP has organized a "National Employer Team," which consists of companies that have made a strong commitment to hiring and retaining older workers.[23]

Other companies are taking very specific actions to recruit mature workers. L.L.Bean targets senior centers and staffs job fairs that tend to attract older workers. Ads targeting older workers often mention the benefit that the age group most values: flexibility. The company has even experimented, with great success, with an ad that reads, "Use our employee discount to shop for your grandkids." Vanguard analyzed its recruitment materials and discovered that much of its materials showed diverse faces—in terms of gender, ethnicity, and race—but not older faces. The company revamped its materials so that mature workers could see themselves in the company literature. Similarly, Australian bank Westpac revamped its ads to help ensure that older workers felt welcome to apply for jobs there. One recent ad made this explicit: "We all get older—but at Westpac that's not a barrier to getting a job."[24]

Adecco's Renaissance Program is an umbrella program under which all of the company's outreach to experienced workers is housed. The temporary services agency is targeting experienced workers by partnering with some twelve hundred churches and community centers in addition to attending AARP job fairs. More interestingly, company management, acknowledging age bias in the workplace, does "PR" for older workers with its clients, touting the skills and expertise inherent among older employees. "Our clients want high-quality employees," says Joyce Russell, president of Adecco, "and we define quality in terms of people who are grounded, who can make contributions right away, who have a good work ethic, and who know how to integrate quickly into a team. The people who have these skills tend to be those with experience."[25] To combat possible age bias, Adecco counsels its mature workers to dispel stereotypes right away during job interviews. The company spreads the same message to experienced workers themselves. "Many people over fifty are fearful of age discrimination and won't

---

Additional Resources for Managing the Older Workforce

The Conference Board provides a database about older worker practices that allows one to search for a specific practice and find employers that use it, as well as articles about that practice. See http://www.conference-board.org/knowledge/knowledgeDB/matureWorkforce.cfm. A quick review of some of these articles produced this sample list of best practices and employers that demonstrate them:

- Examples of organizations that make use of over-fifty individuals to improve society are described in a publication by the MetLife Foundation and Civic Ventures; see http://www.civicventures.org/breakthrough/reports/BTAreport.pdf.

- RetirementJobs.com, in addition to its main role of providing an online job board for older workers, interviews employers that post jobs to identify their practices. It has a Certified Age Friendly Employer program to identify those employers that follow ten key practices for creating a good work environment for older individuals.

- AARP maintains a range of resources on all issues associated with mature individuals, and its Employer Resource Center, at http://www.aarp.org/money/work/employer_resource_ctr/, provides lessons from the company winners of the biennial Best Employers for Workers Over 50 competition. Conclusions are presented about recruiting practices, training, flexible schedules, and so forth.

More Options Throughout
One's Career

Phased retirement is a reminder that the traditional career trajectory may no longer be the norm. Deloitte & Touche has pioneered a concept called mass career customization (MCC), a model that encourages continuous collaboration between the employer and the employee to design customized career paths. MCC recognizes that flexibility is just one part of a larger picture. In other words, it's an accommodation, not a solution. The Deloitte framework focuses on four aspects of one's career: pace (how quickly the employee wants to progress to increasing levels of responsibility and authority), workload (the quantity of the work itself), location/schedule (where and when the work gets done), and role (the employee's position, job description, and job responsibilities). Ideally, the employee and their manager will meet on a regular basis to select a balance that best reflects the employee's career objectives at that particular time. Consider, for example, the different stages one goes through in a twenty-year career (see figure).

Ideally, people can move the arrow up or down depending on their life situation. Although MCC is not designed specifically for older workers—in fact, it applies to all workers—it gives companies a way of thinking about phased retirement and how to structure a plan that works for

even bother applying for jobs," says Bernadette Kenney, Adecco's chief career officer. "We need to make sure they don't give up, and recognize the value they bring to the workplace."[26]

Phased Retirement

The most obvious group of mature workers to target for recruiting are those within one's own organization who are about to leave. The

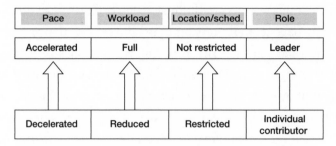

Pace	Workload	Location/sched.	Role
Accelerated	Full	Not restricted	Leader
Decelerated	Reduced	Restricted	Individual contributor

Source: Adapted from Cathleen Benko and Anne Weisberg, "Implementing a Corporate Career Lattice: The Mass Career Customization Model," *Strategy & Leadership* 35, no. 5 (2007): 29–36.

both parties involved. Deloitte piloted MCC with 120 participants in 2005 and again in 2006 with 300 participants. The overall results showed:[a]

- Improved satisfaction with career-life fit

- Positive impact of MCC for nearly 90 percent on their decision to stay with the company

- Maintenance of client service standards

- Achievement of significant savings, mainly through retention

- Improved employee morale, satisfaction, and productivity

a. Cathleen Benko and Anne Weisberg, "Implementing a Corporate Career Lattice: The Mass Career Customization Model," *Strategy & Leadership* 35, no. 5 (2007): 29–36.

idea of a "phased retirement" plays out the interests expressed by most employees in chapter 1, that they would prefer to withdraw from work gradually rather than all at once. (And phased retirement is only one option. See "More Options Throughout One's Career.") What that means in practice is a reduction in responsibilities or in hours of work, a transition to other roles in the organization that are different—possibly less demanding, possibly providing different opportunities for contributions. One of the main constraints to a gradual retirement in the past has been restrictions around pensions. As noted earlier, traditional defined benefit pension plans based the payouts to retirees on their compensation in the last few years of their careers. The problem with a phased retirement, therefore, is that a reduction in responsibilities or a transition to less demanding roles invariably comes with a reduction in pay, which then translates into substantially reduced pension benefits. In some cases, whatever the employee earned in additional pay from working longer through a phased retirement is actually offset by the loss in pension benefits.

There is nothing about pension plans per se that requires that benefits be based on pay levels in the last few years. And fewer employers offer defined benefit plans now, which are the only ones where the penalty for phased retirement could apply. As a practical matter, therefore, this constraint on phased retirement is fading and will more or less disappear in the future.

In the meantime, most employers that have pensions with this potential penalty built in have found ways to work around it. The most common approach has been to allow workers to "retire" and take up their company-defined benefit pension and then have an intermediary organization like a temp agency employ the retiree on behalf of their original employer. Because the retiree is not employed by their original employer, their pension is not affected by whatever new level of pay they receive. They can go back to work at their original employer, taking on reduced or redefined roles. We take up this topic in the next section.

Bringing Retirees Back

Keeping mature workers who otherwise would retire on the job longer through gradual or phased reductions in the amount of work they do is an obvious way to engage the mature workforce. Another obvious approach is to bring back employees who have already retired. Employers may not have the opportunities and tasks at the point when an employee is ready to retire to permit a phased retirement, but those opportunities can appear quickly. Bringing back retirees offers all the savings of retaining valuable employees—no hiring and onboarding costs, no training costs, no concerns about culture. And yet they only need to bring back the retirees, and start paying them again, when the need is there.

Programs for staying in touch with workers who have left companies are not new. Companies like Citibank, McKinsey, and Chubb Insurance were well known as far back as the 1950s for maintaining relationships with "alumni" of their firms. More recently, the interest in alumni shifted from using them as a source for business contacts to considering them as candidates to be rehired (see "Social Software Keeps Retirees Connected to the Company" earlier). A great many companies now maintain alumni portals on their Web sites as a means to keep former employees engaged and "in the loop" with the company's plans. It's a natural extension to do the same thing with retirees. Con Edison in New York City includes its retirees in solicitations for the company's volunteer corps, community outreach programs in which employees participate, leveraging the company's investments in community activities.

The most common arrangement for bringing back retirees is as a just-in-time workforce, coming back on a temporary basis to help meet peak work demands or to staff unexpected projects. These just-in-time workers provide the perfect solution to the talent management challenge most companies now face, and that is how to respond to unexpected changes in business demands that would otherwise break the bank. Companies are under pressure to staff up quickly when business spikes so as not to miss opportunities for grabbing profits and market share. At the same time, the staff required to capture those opportunities are incredibly expensive if they have to be carried through downturns when business demands have declined and there is nothing for them to do. The alternative of trying to operate with lean staffing and then ramp up quickly when business picks up is very difficult given the costs of outside job searching, the time and money required to train new employees, the inevitable risk of bad hires, and the concern that bringing in lots of new employees all at once can change the culture of an organization.

Bringing back retired workers to help meet these spikes in demand is therefore incredibly cost effective for the employer. Cigna, for example, has been bringing back its retirees for the past twenty years with its Encore Program.[27] The program was the brainchild of the then executive vice president of HR, who wondered why the company was letting go of its most knowledgeable employees. Cigna retirees can work up to eighty hours per month and remain in the Encore Program. They are considered hourly part-time employees and as such can receive retiree medical insurance coverage (if they have worked a minimum number of years) and can contribute to their 401(k) plans. Monsanto's Retiree Resource Corps is one of the most sophisticated of these programs in that it is built around an advanced database outlining the skills and competencies of its retirees who want to work part-time, full-time, or on special assignment. Retirees can join after having been out of regular employment for six months. The program, started in 1991, has three hundred people in the database, with about two hundred on assignment now at twelve Monsanto operations nationwide.[28] The company claims the program has saved $600,000 just in fees that otherwise would have been paid to temp agencies.[29] Georgia Power and MITRE have similar programs.

Using retirees as a contingent workforce also helps employers expand when the upturn in demand is permanent. Retirees can get projects under way while permanent hires are being brought on board.

Perhaps the most interesting arrangement for bringing back retirees operates between companies. Procter & Gamble and Eli Lilly created YourEncore in 2003, an independent company with an online database of retired research scientists and engineers from the two companies, in order to offer short-term R&D contracts to them.

Boeing and National Starch and Chemical later joined YourEncore.[30] The big advantage of this consortium approach is that it lets participating companies draw from an even bigger pool of talent than they have among their own retirees. A participating employer can use the retiree pool essentially as consultants, not only to bolster current competencies but to advance new ones. YourEncore recruits the retirees, contracts with the employers, and sends the retirees out on short-term assignments with the participating companies. Retirees are paid based on their salaries at the time of retirement, so it's not a low-wage operation.

Special Recognition and Acknowledgment

The surveys of older worker interests and preferences described earlier make it clear that psychological rewards from work are especially important for them. And several organizations have begun to pay attention to those rewards. It was common in the workplace to celebrate long-service anniversaries a generation ago, but then most companies abandoned the practice. Now some are bringing it back. CVS, for example, celebrates these service anniversaries, recognizing *total* years of employment, not just those at CVS, and also publishes a maturity-focused publication and newsletter articles lauding the productivity and effectiveness of its older employees.[31] Bon Secours Richmond Health System now does something similar for older workers with long-service anniversary celebrations.[32]

We would be remiss for not acknowledging the enormous and rich literature in geriatrics that discusses impairments that are common among older individuals and how they might be addressed through workplace accommodations.[33] It is worth noting, of course, that not all older workers have these problems, and it is best to address needs on an individual basis. Under U.S. employment law, employers are required to make reasonable accommodations for all workers who have disabilities, not just older workers.

Conclusion

Perhaps the most important conclusion about how to attract and manage older workers is that the practices and policies that work best are ones that have general appeal to all workers. Every HR and benefits manager interviewed for this book echoed this sentiment, saying that their goal was to offer programs that appealed to a wide swath of employees, even if it appealed to them for different reasons. An older employee, for example, might appreciate flexibility in order to travel or spend time with grandchildren, while flexibility might appeal to parents of toddlers or school-age children for very different reasons. This is reflected in AARP's Best Employers for Workers Over 50 program, which does not require employers to have programs dedicated exclusively to mature workers. The rationale here is that what's good for mature workers is often good for all workers.

A second conclusion, more of a surprise, is that many of the attributes about jobs and workplaces that are most important for older workers are also ones that are especially important for young workers. These include a sense of mission concerning the overall goals of the organization, interest in social relationships, and work-life balance. One way to think about this result is that the "odd group out" here is not older workers but those in the middle. Something seems to happen to workers as they approach middle age and then fades as they grow older, and that is the growing need for money as we acquire families and take on the responsibilities typically associated with adult life. It is important for employers to pay attention to those needs. But as the older workforce grows, it is also important to recognize the fact that their interests matter as well and in fact are shared by all employees, especially younger workers, who seem to be the focus of popular attention. Finding ways to address their needs does not conflict with the interests of middle-aged workers, either. So it should be a win-win for all sides.

7

Making an Older Workforce Work for You

Throughout this book, we have analyzed the older worker phenomenon, dispelled myths about older workers, made the business case for retaining and hiring older workers, explored the impact of ageism, discussed how to help younger supervisors manage older employees, and suggested ways in which employers can develop policies and practices that meet the needs of older workers. In this chapter, we explore two additional factors that have important implications for employers as they seek to make an age-diverse workforce productive and effective for their companies and organizations: changing marketplace demographics and public policies that impact older workers.

Changing Marketplace Demographics

In chapter 1, we identified three key reasons why there will be more older workers than ever before: (1) aging boomers are causing a dramatic increase in the number of older people, (2) people are living longer, more productive lives, and (3) more and more people are choosing to remain in the workforce longer, or to return to work in some capacity after having retired (out of either choice or necessity). While these factors are fueling an older workforce, they are also creating an older marketplace.

And just as myths and misperceptions about older workers hinder employers' efforts to retain, hire, and manage an older workforce, the myths and misperceptions about older consumers also hinder companies' and other organizations' ability market to and provide products and services to this growing and increasingly influential market.

Simply put, not only are older people leading a demographic revolution that is changing the way we think about aging (including work), they are leading a consumer revolution that is changing the way we do business. The more that employers understand this connection and the implications it has for their business and their workforce, the better positioned they will be to take advantage of this growing and increasingly lucrative market. After all, how can you reach and serve this market effectively if you don't have at least some people like them—who understand their wants, needs, and lifestyles—in your workforce?

This point was demonstrated in a TV commercial where a fifty-something woman laments that she can't tolerate one more eighteen-year-old girl trying to sell her makeup. This ad rings true for much of today's older population. They want products, services, and experiences that relate to them, that speak to their values and lifestyles, and that demonstrate an understanding of—in fact, an empathy for—their wants and needs.

Just as in chapter 2 we dispelled the myths surrounding older workers, we must also recognize and dispel the myths about older consumers. In *Fifty Plus: Give Meaning and Purpose to the Best Time of Your Life*, Bill Novelli put to rest four key myths:[1]

- Older consumers are reluctant to part with their money.

- Older consumers already have everything they need, so they limit their purchases to replacement items.

- Older consumers resist switching brands more than younger consumers do.

- Older consumers are technophobic.

The fact is, people fifty and older are the new consumer-spending majority in this country. They control much of the country's wealth—70 percent—and in many categories, over 50 percent of consumption.

Collectively, they pull in more than $2 trillion in annual income, account for 50 percent of all discretionary income, and are house-rich: more than 75 percent of people over fifty own their homes—free and clear in nearly 70 percent of those cases.

This isn't to say that all older consumers are wealthy (one-quarter of them make $25,000 a year or less and have little savings), but as a group, the boomers are our wealthiest generation. They continue to have high aspirations and expectations for their lives as they age. These aspirations, combined with their openness to new ideas, are generating new and exciting opportunities for businesses that will continue into the coming decades. The convergence of longer life expectancy and rapid technological advances is sweeping away the perception that the second half of life is a time of gradual decline.

We see the impact of this in the emergence of older people as the new consumer-spending majority. As Steve Gillon observed in his book, *Boomer Nation*, "At heart the boomers were consumers, not revolutionaries."[2]

Spending is often spurred by life transition events such as divorce, remarriage, a birth or death in the family, kids leaving home, adult children moving back in, or the acceptance of caregiving responsibilities for elderly parents. These types of events are more frequent for people in their fifties than at any other age.

For most people, these are also their peak earning years, and people fifty and older not only earn more money, they also spend more of it than marketers have traditionally believed. While the recent recession has put a crimp in all consumer spending, the demographics of aging indicate that older consumers will continue to be a dominant force as consumer spending rises again. These older consumers account for at least half the sales of women's apparel, appliances, housing, groceries, take-out food, entertainment, health insurance, and new cars and trucks. They buy three-fourths of all prescription drugs and about half of over-the-counter (OTC) medications. They also purchase 25 percent of all toys and account for a 21 percent increase over the past three years in the rate at which people join health clubs. And new markets are emerging for senior housing and senior care, all linked to new living, working, and retirement patterns.

The market for home-office supplies and furniture is also growing, as is the market for new and affordable technology. Why? Because since 1995, the fifty-and-over age group has been the fastest-growing segment of home-based businesses, with people putting their experience and talents to work for themselves. This exciting trend toward entrepreneurship is lucrative for the marketers of laptop computers, wireless Internet service, e-mail, fax machines, copiers, scanners, cell phones, pagers, BlackBerrys, phone company–based voice mail, and the like.

Yet, all work and no play is hardly the anthem for these vital, active, and involved people. They want to experience life to the fullest, and that includes having fun, especially when it revolves around new experiences.

Not surprisingly, travel ranks high on the list; this age group travels more than any other. They account for 70 percent of all cruise passengers and 72 percent of all recreational vehicle trips. The Travel Industry Association of America predicts fivefold growth in the global travel industry's income over the next two decades. People fifty and over are also willing to dig deep into their pockets to make the most of the travel experience. On a typical vacation, they spend

74 percent more than younger travelers, and when they can afford it, they go first class: 80 percent of all high-end travel and 65 percent of cruises are by those fifty and older.[3]

Changing social roles at different stages of life also influence consumer behavior. For example, there are 60 million grandparents in the United States—72 percent of Americans age fifty and over are grandparents. The average age of a first-time grandparent in the United States is only forty-eight. But whatever their age, grandparents tend to dote on their grandkids.

They spend time and money—over $30 billion annually—on them. More than ever before, grandparents are taking their grandchildren along to restaurants and other outings. So-called *grand travel*, in which grandparents take the grandchildren but not the kids' parents on vacation, is also gaining in popularity. Disney certainly knows and cares about this phenomenon. Other companies do, too.

Honda thought its minivans were just for under-fifty soccer moms. The company's assumption was that once the kids were grown, these buyers would move up to fancier Acura models. Instead, Honda discovered that 40 percent of its minivan buyers were empty nesters, mostly boomers, who wanted roomy vehicles to carry grandchildren, elderly parents, and all those home-repair materials from The Home Depot and Lowe's.

Honda responded by introducing an upgraded Odyssey minivan outfitted with leather seats and featuring zoned climate control and other pricey features that appeal to wealthier, older buyers with an active lifestyle.

For business leaders, the message is obvious: disregard at your own peril the expanding fifty-and-over group that buys boatloads of products and services, frequently eats in restaurants, goes to movies, stays in hotels, works out at the gym, travels, builds new homes (or renovates existing ones), rents cars, goes back to school, engages in civic ventures, and is eager for new adventures.

According to McKinsey & Company's U.S. Aging Consumer Initiative, the increased spending by older consumers will account for the vast majority of total spending increases over the next ten years in many categories, including medical fees and services, food at home, prescription drugs, food away from home, health and beauty aids (OTC), housewares, furniture and appliances, clothing and accessories, footwear, jewelry, apparel services, and consumer electronics. America's older consumers will also hold more than 50 percent market share in all of these categories except clothing and accessories (48 percent) and footwear, jewelry, and apparel services (44 percent).

This creates enormous opportunities for companies and organizations that are prepared to address the wants and needs of older consumers, especially boomers. These include:

- *Redefining active retirement.* As economic necessity and personal choice drive boomers to work longer, employers with innovative approaches for recruiting and retaining boomers will have an edge in meeting the growing need for knowledge workers.

- *Protecting wealth and health.* As boomers confront their financial and physical health, they will seek products and services that are more trustworthy and offer them more control than traditional solutions, which many reject.

- *Serving unprepared, underfunded boomers.* Winning companies will create new solutions that meet these underfunded, discriminating consumers' expectations for price, service, and convenience (think JetBlue).

- *Creating community.* Like previous generations, boomers do want to find community in family, friends, and religion, and companies can create additional communities through the Internet, new travel options, socially conscious work, and retail shopping occasions.

Implications

All of this has significant implications for employers in terms of workforce and markets. What we know about older consumers— their wants and needs, their behaviors, and how they view life going forward—tells us that employers also need to look at their older employees differently. Age is not the only discerning factor. While employers often view them as "older workers," AARP research indicates that these older employees do not focus on their age. They tend to view life (and work) as a progression and resent attempts to label them or to put them in a box. They're more focused on where they are in life and what's next. By taking a holistic view of their employees, and discounting aging stereotypes, employers will be better able to relate and respond to their wants and needs. For example, by relating to them more from the standpoint of where they are in life and the stage where they are in their careers, employers may get a better sense of which working arrangements and benefits would work best for these employees than they would by making assumptions based on age alone.

In order to take advantage of a growing older marketplace that until recently has largely been ignored, employers need innovation grounded in experience. This is best accomplished by employing more older workers, thus creating a more diverse, multigenerational workforce.

In a recent article in the *European Journal of Marketing,* authors Nicholas J. Thompson and Keith E. Thompson make the point that as a result of the demographic shift toward older consumers, marketing also will have to shift away from its youth-oriented approach toward a more customercentric model of marketing.[4]

In making this shift, however, marketers will also need to understand that older consumers are not all alike. Research by Focalyst for AARP identified five distinct segments of boomers, each of which differs significantly on a number of variables, including health, finances, shopping attitudes, household makeup, how they use and relate to media and advertising, and the general activities they enjoy.[5] This view is also supported by research published in the *Journal of Consumer Marketing*, in which the authors found five distinct segments that differ from one another on a range of variables, including consumer behavior.[6]

Given these trends, employers need to look at their own organizations and consider:

- What is the generational composition of my current workforce? What will it/should it be in five years?

- What is the generational composition of my customer base? What will it be in five years?

So what conclusions can employers draw from all of this? First, it is important to understand older people, not just as older workers but also as customers. Determine what role older people play in your organization, what role you want them to play in the future, and what your value proposition should be. Finally, in reviewing your product and service portfolio, consider the fifty-and-over market, including the rise of boomer spending, and invest now to develop new products and services to address the wants and needs of this population.

Public Policies That Impact Older Workers

As is evident throughout the previous chapters, there can be great benefits to both employers and employees when workers stay in the workforce longer. It is also beneficial to our society as a whole. This raises the question, what can be done through public policies to help facilitate this process?

There is no question that work is a crucial component of financial security later in life. We cannot escape the fact that people will

TABLE 7-1

Working longer reduces the total assets needed in retirement

Retirement age	80% of preretirement after-tax income	Annual social security payments	Additional annual income needed to achieve 80% replacement	Assets needed at age 62 to produce that additional income at retirement
62	$46,848	$20,088	$26,760	$510,757
66	$46,848	$27,648	$19,200	$243,340
70	$46,848	$38,136	$8,712	$51,768

Source: Congressional Budget Office, Retirement Age and the Need for Saving, Economic and Budget Issue Brief, May 12, 2004, Table 1.

Note: These examples assume households with income levels that are roughly the median for working married couples ages 55–64. The figures are based on the cost of an annuity from the federal Thrift Savings Plan. For married couples, it is a joint and 50 percent survivor's annuity. It assumes a savings rate of 10 percent between age 62 and retirement age, and a real (inflation-adjusted) rate of return of 3 percent.

need to work longer in the future to achieve their retirement security goals. Today, the age at which the most people retire is just over sixty-two. This cannot be sustained without putting an entire generation of retirees at risk of inadequate incomes, depriving our economy of highly skilled and productive workers, and putting tremendous stress on our national deficits and debt. Table 7-1 illustrates the impact of working longer on the total assets needed for retirement.

The following public policy options identify strategies for keeping people in the workforce longer while protecting people who cannot continue to work.

Training and Retraining

In a rapidly changing global economy, frequent training and retraining is increasingly necessary if workers of any age are to remain employable. Older workers in particular are at risk of skills obsolescence.

Much can be done in the private sector to enhance opportunities for job training, but public policy solutions are also needed. Federal funding for training, including training for groups with special labor market needs (such as older workers), could be increased. Tax laws could be amended to permit workers to deduct all appropriate expenses for job-related training and retraining to acquire skills for a new trade or business. Specifically, an above-the-line educational deduction on the IRS Form 1040 for legitimate training and educational expenses not subject to the 2 percent of adjusted gross income (AGI) floor on itemized deductions might encourage workers to acquire skills for a new trade or business.

Promoting Flexible Work Arrangements

About 50 percent of workers take Social Security at age sixty-two, and about two-thirds take it before age sixty-five. Given expected increases in longevity, that pattern is not sustainable over the long term either for the Social Security system or for individual retirement security. As a nation, we need to move from the current situation to a more sustainable balance between years spent working and years spent in retirement. We need to take increased longevity into account. To reach this new balance, we must eliminate—or at the least, substantially reduce—age discrimination, which hampers the ability of workers to remain in the labor force. We need to create age-neutral workplaces with adequate job options for older workers. To promote both job availability and job satisfaction, we also need to increase job flexibility by moving from one-size-fits-all schedules to more flexible, adaptable jobs.

As we have demonstrated throughout this book, the twenty-first-century workforce is very different from the twentieth-century workforce. Dual-earner couples are the norm; older workers need to work longer to save for retirement; men and women often share caregiving responsibilities; there are many more single-parent families; many lower-wage workers have nonstandard work schedules and multiple jobs to make ends meet; and more people with disabilities are working, but many need a range of support.

Despite this increased diversity and complexity within the American workforce—and the intensifying global competition in a 24/7 marketplace—our workplaces have not caught up in a systematic or sophisticated way with these new realities. We live in a world of changing social patterns but often unyielding institutions.

Workplace Flexibility 2010, a public policy initiative at Georgetown University Law Center that is the lead policy component of the Alfred P. Sloan Foundation's National Initiative on Workplace Flexibility, views workplace flexibility as part of the solution to many of the intense pressures facing American employees and employers. The leaders of this initiative are currently developing a range of public policy solutions on workplace flexibility—including flexible work arrangements, time off, and career maintenance and reentry—that work for both employers and employees. As we have pointed out, one of the desires of many older workers, where feasible, is to have flexibility in work schedules.

Promoting Phased Retirement to Employers and Workers

Many older workers say they expect and/or want to work later in life—and many are doing so—but not all of them want to work full-time. As discussed in the previous chapter, one solution is to implement phased retirement programs.

If phased retirement options are to become more widely available, changes in public policy and actions by employers are needed. The Pension Protection Act of 2006 has made it possible for workers to receive in-service pensions at age sixty-two. But other impediments to phased retirement remain and may require amendments to the tax code, the Employee Retirement Income Security Act (ERISA), and the Age Discrimination in Employment Act (ADEA) in order to relax certain nondiscrimination rules and protect employers from the risk of ADEA lawsuits. At the same time, employers could be required to offer phased retirees the same benefits, on a prorated basis, that are offered to full-time workers.

Public policy changes can be accelerated by employer advocacy. Many corporations and their trade associations are active in these endeavors, and this participation in legislative and regulatory reforms is an important way to create opportunities for a stronger American workforce. Although it is tempting to avoid engagement in Washington and state policy advocacy and lobbying, business leaders should realize that their actions in this arena shape how well they do as corporations and how well we do as a society.

Promoting Healthy-Worker Initiatives

Encouraging older workers to remain in the workforce by enhancing work options is essential for lengthening work lives to increase retirement security. Yet, another critical element is providing incentives to employers to retain and hire older workers, who are often seen, however incorrectly, as costing more and being less productive than younger workers. The key factor most often cited for not doing this is health-care costs, which many employers believe can raise the costs of older workers to employers, a misperception we refuted in chapter 2.

One way to address this is to incentivize employers, through changes in public policy, to offer more programs that address wellness issues (e.g., smoking cessation, weight loss, exercise, nutrition counseling). This would also help employers to recognize that age is not as much a predictor of employee cost as health status is. Such programs appear to be increasing among employers, and there is growing evidence that they reduce health costs and possibly increase productivity among all employees, regardless of age.

Another potential policy solution is through federal reinsurance of high-cost health-care claims. The goal of reinsurance in the small-group and individual markets is to discourage risk selection by reducing the risk of high costs to individual insurers. Pooling the risk to individual insurers by having the government reinsure companies against catastrophic costs would in theory reduce premiums by reducing the amount set aside for risk capital. This could reduce cost volatility and perhaps translate into more stable premiums and, thus, more stability in coverage. This is especially important for older workers, who tend to have more chronic conditions and diseases that require more treatment.

Conclusion

Having workers remain in the workforce longer as productive employees has significant benefits for our society. It helps employers avert potential labor shortages and receive the contributions of experienced, reliable, and knowledgeable people. It helps individuals meet their needs for income during their later years and provide for continued productive engagement in society. And older workers continue to earn money in addition to their public and private pensions. And while they are getting their retirement benefits, their wages and salaries are still subject to FICA withholding, so they continue to pay into a system that is paying them.

As we have attempted to demonstrate throughout, employers, government, and employees themselves all have key roles and responsibilities for making this happen. Government has a responsibility to continue enforcing laws against age discrimination in the workplace and can support a new vision of work in retirement by providing incentives for employers to hire older workers and for individuals to continue working. Individuals have a responsibility to remain employable by updating and learning new skills and ways of working. And employers can implement best practices and gain competitive advantages by retaining and recruiting older workers.

All this constitutes change in the way our workforce is organized and managed. Twenty-five years ago (more recently, in some industries and sectors), a key question being asked and pondered among many male workers was, "Can I report to a woman?" Today, in virtually every sector of our society, the question has been answered in the affirmative. We have women running corporations, large and small. University presidents and deans are women. Women are overseeing sports teams, military units, and major nonprofit organizations. Women MBAs are proliferating. We have many women in key government positions, including cabinet members, governors, and mayors. They are leading and managing, and the idea of a man reporting to a woman is virtually a nonissue.

Now the question that may be asked among older workers is, "Can I report to a younger person?" More specifically, "At age sixty-five or seventy, am I going to be able to work for a young person who is half my age and has less than half my experience?" We believe that the answer will again be in the affirmative. It is happening more and more, and it will become even more commonplace as the demographics continue to shift. But as we have pointed out, it will take change: in the way managers lead and teach, in the way they present expectations and conduct performance reviews. And it will take skills and a willingness to accept a new order of things among older workers. It can all be done, and the result can be a better, stronger, more productive workforce.

By coming together and working toward a common vision with shared goals, different stakeholders can have a tremendous impact on society while benefiting employers and employees alike.

Notes

Chapter 1

1. For the classic discussion of this issue, see Richard Easterlin, *Birth and Fortune* (Chicago: University of Chicago Press 1980).

2. See, e.g., U.S. Bureau of the Census, Table 2b, "Projected Populations Change in the United States, by Age and Sex: 2000–2050," http://www.census.gov/ipc/www/usinterimproj/natprojtab02b.pdf.

3. National Center for Health Statistics, U.S. Department of Health and Human Services, *Health, United States, 2006* (Washington, DC: U.S. Department of Health and Human Services, 2006), http://www.cdc.gov/nchs/data/hus/hus06.pdf#027.

4. John B. Shoven, "New Age Thinking: Alternative Ways of Measuring Age, Their Relationship to Labor Force Participation, Government Policies and GDP." (working paper 13476, National Bureau of Economic Research, Cambridge, MA, October 2007).

5. The bulge of the baby boom—a disproportionately large cohort that is getting older—complicates this conclusion as it adds so many more individuals into the category of chronologically old. After the proportion of those over age sixty-five begins to slow, however, the proportion of the population defined by remaining years of life expectancy begins to decline.

6. Chinhui Juhn and Simon Potter, "Changes in Labor Force Participation in the United States," *Journal of Economic Perspectives* 20, no. 3 (2006): 27–46.

7. Shoven, "New Age Thinking."

8. Gordon B. T. Mermin, Richard W. Johnson, and Dan P. Murphy, "Why Do Boomers Plan to Work Longer? *Journals of Gerontology Series B: Psychological Sciences & Social Sciences* 62B, no. 5 (2007): S286–S294.

9. See Dora L. Costa, *The Evolution of Retirement: An American Economic History, 1880–1990* (Chicago: University of Chicago Press, 1998).

10. Cited in Robert Hutchens and Karen Grace-Martin, "Employer Willingness to Permit Phased Retirement: Why Are Some More Willing Than Others?" *Industrial and Labor Relations Review* 59, no. 4 (2006): 525–546.

11. David Blau and Tetyana Shvydko, "Labor Market Rigidities and the Employment Behavior of Older Workers" (working paper CES-WP-07-21, U.S. Census Bureau, Center for Economic Studies).

12. Katherine G. Abraham and Susan N. Houseman, "Work and Retirement Plans Among Older Americans," in *Reinventing the Retirement Paradigm,* eds. Robert L. Clark and Olivia S. Mitchell (New York: Oxford University Press, 2005), 70–91.

13. Maximiliane E. Szinovacz and Adam Davey, "Predictors of Perceptions of Involuntary Retirement," *Gerontologist* 45, no. 1 (2005): 36–47.

14. Ruth Helman, Craig Copeland, and Jack VanDerhei, *Will More of Us Be Working Forever? The 2006 Retirement Confidence Survey* (Washington, DC: Employee Benefit Research Institute, 2006), http://www.ebri.org/pdf/EBRI_IB_04-2006_1.pdf.

15. Phyllis Moen et al., "A Life Course Approach to Retirement and Social Integration," in *Social Integration in the Second Half of Life,* eds. K. Pillemer et al. (Baltimore: Johns Hopkins Press, 2000).

16. Julie Zissimopolous and Lynn A. Karoly, *Work and Well-Being Among the Self-Employed at Older Ages* (Washington, DC: AARP, 2007).

17. See Mitra Toossi, "Labor Force Projections to 2014: Retiring Boomers," *Monthly Labor Review* 128, no. 11 (2005). These forecasts are difficult to do. To put the 0.20 percent projected decline in perspective, the error rate in the previous BLS forecasts of labor force growth have been about 0.10 percent six years or so out. See Howard N. Fullerton Jr., "Evaluating the BLS Labor Force Projections to 2000," *Monthly Labor Review* 126, no. 10 (2003).

18. Mitra Toossi, "Labor Force Projections to 2016: More Workers in Their Golden Years," *Monthly Labor Review* 130, no. 11 (2007).

19. For sober and consistent views on the future labor force and its effect on the economy, see Richard B. Freeman, "Is a Great Labor Shortage Coming? Replacement Demand in the Global Economy" (working paper 12541, National Bureau of Economic Research, Cambridge, MA, September 2006); and Peter Cappelli, "Will There *Really* Be a Labor Shortage?" *Organizational Dynamics,* no. 3 (2003).

20. Watson Wyatt Worldwide, *Effect of the Economic Crisis on Employee Attitudes Toward Retirement, Part II: Retirement Timing* (Arlington, VA: Watson Wyatt Worldwide, 2009).

21. See Alan L. Gustman and Thomas L. Steinmeier, "Retirement and the Stock Market Bubble" (working paper 9404, National Bureau of Economic Research, Cambridge, MA, 2002), http://www.nber.org/papers/w9404.

Chapter 2

1. Center for Retirement Research, Boston College, "The National Retirement Risk Index in a Nutshell," http://crr.bc.edu/images/stories/NRRI_Files/nrrinutshell.pdf?phpMyAdmin=43ac483c4de9t51d9eb41.

2. For a summary of these projections, see Katharine Bradbury, Christopher L. Foote, and Robert K. Triest, *Labor Supply in the New Century* (Boston: Federal Reserve Bank, 2008).

3. "Staying Ahead of the Curve: The AARP Work and Career Study," survey conducted by RoperASW (Washington, DC: AARP, 2002).

4. *Staying Ahead of the Curve: The AARP Work and Career Study,* national survey conducted for AARP by RoperASW, September 2002, http://assets.aarp.org/rgcenter/econ/d17773_multiwork_1.pdf.

5. Ibid.

6. Phyllis Moen, "Not So Big Jobs and Retirements: What Workers (and Retirees) Really Want," *Generations* 31, no. 1 (2007): 31–36.

7. David Autor and David Dorn, "This Job Is 'Getting Old': Measuring Changes in Job Opportunities Using Occupational Age Structure," *American Economic Review* 99, no. 2 (2009): 45–51.

8. There are limits to the idea that experience is the only issue, of course. Some evidence suggests that in certain contexts younger surgeons might perform better, although here it is not that experience hurts but that younger surgeons are better at solving novel problems. See J. F. Waljee et al., "Surgeon Age and Operative Mortality in the United States," *Annals of Surgery* 244 (2006): 353–362.

9. J. L. Horn, "The Theory of Fluid and Crystallized Intelligence in Relation to Concepts of Cognitive Psychology and Aging in Adulthood," in *Aging and Cognitive Processes,* eds. F. I. M. Craik and S. Trehub (New York: Plenum Press, 1982), 237–278.

10. Research seems to point to the declines in the dopamine system in the prefrontal cortex as causing declines in episodic memory and working memory as well as "executive function." The ability to repress unnecessary information and control our focus of attention also declines, affecting the ability to understand context and maintain information. See T. S. Braver et al., "Context Processing in Older Adults: Evidence for a Theory Relating

Cognitive Control to Neurobiology in Healthy Aging," *Journal of Experimental Psychology: General* 130 (2001): 746–763.

11. N. Unsworth and R. W. Engle, "The Nature of Individual Differences in Working Memory Capacity: Active Maintenance in Primary Memory and Controlled Search from Secondary Memory," *Psychological Review* 114 (2007):104–132.

12. S. Hale and J. Myerson, "Fifty Years Older, Fifty Percent Slower? Meta-analytic Regression Models and Semantic Context Effects," *Aging and Cognition* 2 (1995): 132–145. See also Sara J. Czaja and Joseph Sharit, *Aging and Work: Issues and Implications in a Changing Landscape.* (Baltimore: Johns Hopkins University Press, 2009).

13. J. L. Taylor et al., "Cognitive Ability, Expertise, and Age Differences in Following Air-Traffic Control Instructions," *Psychology and Aging* 20 (2005): 117–133.

14. D. E. Mireles and N. Charness, "Computational Explorations of the Influence of Structured Knowledge on Age-Related Cognitive Decline," *Psychology and Aging* 17 (2002): 245–259.

15. D. K. Simonton, "Creative Productivity: A Predictive and Explanatory Model of Career Trajectories and Landmarks," *Psychological Review* 104 (1997): 66–89.

16. G. M. McEvoy and W. F. Cascio, "Cumulative Evidence of the Relationship Between Employee Age and Job Performance," *Journal of Applied Psychology* 74 (1989): 11–17; and M. C. Sturman, "Searching for the Inverted U-Shaped Relationship Between Time and Performance: Meta-analyses of the Experience/Performance, Tenure/Performance, and Age/Performance Relationships," *Journal of Management* 29 (2004): 609–640.

17. J. E. Kubeck et al., "Does Job-Related Training Performance Decline with Age?" *Psychology and Aging* 11 (1996): 92–107.

18. N. Charness et al., "Word Processing Training and Retraining: Effects of Adult Age, Experience, and Interface," *Psychology and Aging* 16 (2001): 110–127.

19. In fact, the variability of performance in older workers is greater for more challenging tasks. See P. Shammi, E. Bosman, and D. T. Stuss, "Aging and Variability in Performance," *Aging, Neuropsychology, and Cognition* 5 (1998): 1–13.

20. See, e.g., T. M. Hess, "Memory and Aging in Context," *Psychological Bulletin* 131, no. 3 (2005): 383–406.

21. R. Kliegl, J. Smith, and P. B. Baltes, "Testing-the-Limits and the Study of Adult Age Differences in Cognitive Plasticity of a Mnemonic Skill," *Developmental Psychology* 25 (1989): 247–256.

22. Bureau of Labor Statistics, "Table 2. Median Usual Weekly Earnings of Full-Time Wage and Salary Workers by Age, Race, Hispanic or Latino Ethnicity, and Sex, Fourth Quarter 2007 Averages, Not Seasonally Adjusted," Economic News Release, http://www.bls.gov/news.release/wkyeng.t02.htm.

23. See, e.g., Judith K. Hellerstein, David Neumark, and Kenneth R. Troske, "Wages, Productivity and Worker Characteristics: Evidence from Plant-Level Production Functions and Wage Equations," *Journal of Labor Economics* 17, no. 3 (1999): 409–446.

24. An interesting issue for speculation is whether the increased supply of older and experienced workers will cause the premium for experience to decline. For a discussion, see Bradbury, Foote, and Triest, *Labor Supply in the New Century.*

25. Keith W. Chauvin, "Firm-Specific Wage Growth and Changes in the Labor Market for Managers," *Managerial and Decision Economics* 15, no. 1 (January–February 1994): 21–37.

26. Claire Brown, ed., *The Competitive Semiconductor Manufacturing Human Resources Project* (Berkeley: University of California, 1997).

27. David Marcotte, "The Wage Premium for Job Seniority During the 1980s and Early 1990s," *Industrial Relations* 37, no. 4 (1998): 419.

28. Joseph G. Altonji and Nicolas Williams, "Do Wages Rise with Job Seniority? A Reassessment," *Industrial and Labor Relations Review* 58, no. 3 (2005): 370–397.

29. It is important to point out, however, that the experience of those who change jobs voluntarily (the majority) is quite different from that of those who are forced to change jobs because they are laid off. The probability that employees who quit will find a job that offers a large pay raise has increased by 5 percent, while the probability that those who are dismissed will suffer a large decline in their pay has risen by 17 percent in the 1990s, as compared with the 1980s; see Daniel Polsky, "Changing Consequences of Job Separations in the United States," *Industrial and Labor Relations Review* 52, no. 4 (July 1999): 565–580.

30. See Andrei Shleifer and Lawrence H. Summers, "Breach of Trust in Hostile Takeovers," in *Corporate Takeovers: Causes and Consequences,* ed. Alan J. Auerbach (Chicago: University of Chicago Press, 1988), 33–67. Evidence that job cuts disproportionately targeted senior employees in hostile takeovers is in Jagadeesh Gokhale, Erica L. Groshen, and David Neumark, "Do Hostile Takeovers Reduce Extramarginal Wage Payments?" *Review of Economics and Statistics* 770, no. 3 (1995): 470–485.

31. *The Business Case for Workers Age 50+: Planning for Tomorrow's Talent Needs in Today's Competitive Environment,* report for AARP prepared by

Towers Perrin, December 2005, http://assets.aarp.org/rgcenter/econ/workers_fifty_plus_1.pdf.

32. Employee Benefit Research Institute (EBRI), "Retiree Health Insurance: Facts and Figures," *Fast Facts from EBRI* (Washington, DC: EBRI, 2006), http://www.ebri.org/pdf/publications/facts/fastfacts/fastfact101707.pdf.

33. EBRI, *EBRI Databook on Employee Benefits: Chapter 27: Health Insurance Coverage of Workers* (Washington, DC: EBRI, October 2007), http://www.ebri.org/pdf/publications/books/databook/DB.Chapter%2027.pdf.

34. This story is described in Gina Ruiz, "Gray Eminence," *Workforce Management,* March 27, 2006, 32–36.

35. National Research Council, *Health and Safety Needs of Older Workers* (Washington, DC: National Academy Press, 2004). Another study examining on-the-job accidents and injuries finds that older workers are less likely to be injured but take longer to heal. See Elizabeth Rogers and William J. Wiatrowski, "Injuries, Illnesses, and Fatalities Among Older Workers," *Monthly Labor Review,* October 2005, http://www.bls.gov/opub/mlr/2005/10/art3full.pdf.

36. J. J. Martocchio, "Age-Related Differences in Employee Absenteeism: A Meta-analysis," *Psychology and Aging* 4 (1989): 409–414.

Chapter 3

1. U.S. Department of Labor, *The Older American Worker: Report of the Secretary of Labor to the Congress Under Section 715 of the Civil Rights Act of 1964* (Washington, DC: U.S. Department of Labor, 1965).

2. These restrictions applied to Social Security as well as pensions, where there was at one point a one-for-one penalty for earned income: every dollar you earned led to a $1 reduction in Social Security payments. Working for pay effectively meant losing pension and Social Security benefits.

3. Lutz Bellmann and Martin Brussig, *Recruitment and Job Applications of Older Jobseekers from the Establishments' Perspective,* Discussion Paper Series (Bonn, Germany: Institute for the Study of Labor, April 2007), IZA DP No. 2721.

4. Robert M. Hutchens, "Do Job Opportunities Decline with Age?" *Industrial and Labor Relations Review* 42, no. 1 (1988): 89–99.

5. The consequences of introducing protections against age discrimination are complicated. For example, those states that introduced such protections actually saw lower rates of employment for those over age fifty. Was the risk of litigation enough to scare employers away from even hiring older workers? See Joanna Lahey, "State Age Protection Laws and the Age

Discrimination in Employment Act" (working paper 12048, National Bureau of Economic Research, Cambridge, MA, February 2006).

6. For a detailed description of these changes, see Peter Cappelli, *The New Deal at Work: Managing the Market-Driven Workforce* (Boston: Harvard Business School Press, 1999).

7. Ryan Helwig, "Worker Displacement in 1999–2000," *Monthly Labor Review* 127, no. 6 (2004): 54–68.

8. Daniel Rodriguez and Madeline Zavodny, "Changes in the Age and Education Profile of Displaced Workers," *Industrial and Labor Relations Review* 56, no. 3 (2003): 498–510.

9. Henry S. Farber, "Job Loss in the United States, 1981–2001" (working paper 471, Princeton University, Industrial Relations Section, 2003).

10. Henry S. Farber, "What Do We Know About Job Loss in the United States? Evidence from the Displaced Workers Survey, 1984–2004," *Economic Perspectives* 29, no. 2 (2005): 13–28.

11. Andrei Schleifer and Lawrence H. Summers, "Breech of Trust in Hostile Takeovers," in *Corporate Takeovers: Causes and Consequences,* ed. Alan J. Auerbach (Chicago: University of Chicago Press, 1988), 33–67. Careful readers will notice a possible disconnect between the idea that it was important to retain workers to recoup the investments in their training and the idea that there were savings from laying off older workers. The argument was that the two effects crossed paths with the most senior workers.

12. This estimate is from Bruce C. Fallick and Charles A. Fleishman, "Employer-to-Employer Flows in the US Labor Market" (working paper, Federal Reserve Board, Washington, DC, 2002).

13. Peter Cappelli and Monika Hamori, Wharton School white paper. 2008. For details on job hopping across employers and the more general breakdown of lifetime employment, see Cappelli, *The New Deal at Work*; and Peter Cappelli, *Talent on Demand: Managing Talent in an Age of Uncertainty* (Boston: Harvard Business Press, 2008), chap. 3.

14. Sara L. Rynes, Marc O. Orlitzky, and Robert Bretz Jr., "Experienced Hiring Versus College Recruiting: Practices and Emerging Trends," *Personnel Psychology* 50, no. 2 (1997): 309–339.

15. *The Older American Worker.*

16. Christopher J. Ruhm, "Secular Changes in the Work and Retirement Patterns of Older Men," *Journal of Human Resources* 30, no. 2 (Spring 1995): 362–385.

17. U.S. Department of Labor, "Number of Jobs Held, Labor Market Activity, and Earnings Growth Among Younger Baby Boomers: Recent Results from a Longitudinal Survey Summary," news release, August 25, 2004,

http://www.bls.gov/nls/. This study and the others in this section rely on the National Longitudinal Surveys.

18. Annette Bernhardt et al., *Divergent Paths: Economic Mobility in the New American Labor Market* (New York: Russell Sage Foundation, 2001).

19. Kevin E. Cahill, Michael D. Giandrea, and Joseph F. Quinn, "Are Traditional Retirements a Thing of the Past? New Evidence on Retirement Patterns and Bridge Jobs" (working paper 384, Bureau of Labor Statistics, U.S. Department of Labor, Washington, DC, 2005).

20. Lisa M. Lynch and Sandra E. Black, "Beyond the Incidence of Employer-Provided Training," *Industrial and Labor Relations Review* 52, no. 1 (1998).

21. Jill L. Constantine and David Neumark, "Training and Growth of Wage Inequality," *Industrial Relations* 35, no. 4 (1996): 491–510.

22. See Tammy Galvin, "2003 Industry Report," *Training* 40, no. 9 (2003). To what extent this decline is simply representative of a recessionary period, recovery from which is expected, or is a secular decline is difficult to say because the survey no longer appears to be conducted.

23. Harley Frazis et al., "Results from the 1995 Survey of Employer-Provided Training," *Monthly Labor Review* 121, no. 6 (1998): 3–13.

24. Deloitte Development LLC, *It's 2008: Do You Know Where Your Talent Is? Why Acquisition and Retention Strategies Don't Work*, 2006.

25. *The Business Case for Workers Age 50+: Planning for Tomorrow's Talent Needs in Today's Competitive Environment*, report for AARP prepared by Towers Perrin, December 2005, http://assets.aarp.org/rgcenter/econ/workers_fifty_plus_1.pdf.

26. Peter Cappelli, *A Study of the Extent of and Potential Causes of Alternative Employment Arrangements: Preliminary Report to the Russell Sage Foundation* (New York: Russell Sage Foundation, 2005).

27. Staffing Industry Analysts, *Staffing Industry Report*, 2004, http://www.staffingindustry.com/issues/sireport.

28. David R. Howell and Edward N. Wolff, "Trends in the Growth And Distribution of Skills in the U.S. Workplace, 1960–1985, Industrial & Labor Relations Review, 44, no. 3 (April 1991): 486–502.

29. Peter Cappelli, "Are Skill Requirements Rising? Evidence for Production and Clerical Workers," *Industrial and Labor Relations Review* 46, no. 3 (April 1993): 515–530.

30. Richard W. Johnson, Gordon B. T. Mermin, and Matthew Resseger, *Employment at Older Ages and the Changing Nature of Work* (Washington, DC: AARP, 2007).

31. Ibid.

32. Michael Handel, *Implications of Information Technology for Employment, Skills, and Wages: A Review of Recent Research* (Arlington, VA: SRI International 2003), http://www.socant.neu.edu/faculty/handel/documents/Handel_IT_Final.pdf.

33. Peter Cappelli, "Rethinking the 'Skills Gap,'" *California Management Review* 37, no. 4 (Summer 1995): 108–124.

34. Ibid.

35. J. D. Mayer, D. Caruso, and P. Salovey, "Emotional Intelligence Meets Traditional Standards for an Intelligence," *Intelligence* 27 (1999): 267–298. In *Emotional Intelligence: Key Readings on the Mayer and Salovey Model*, eds. Peter Salovey, PhD, Marc A. Brackett, PhD, and John D. Mayer (Washington, DC: NPR, Inc.).

36. The real problem here is that few employers provide training that updates IT skills. See Peter Cappelli, "Why Is It So Hard to Find IT Workers?" *Organizational Dynamics*, no. 2 (2001): 87–99.

37. M. Pitt-Catsouphes et al., *The National Study Report: Phase II of the National Study of Business Strategy and Workforce Development*, Research Highlight 04 (Chestnut Hill, MA: The Center on Aging & Work/Workplace Flexibility, 2007), http://agingandwork.bc.edu/documents/RH04_National Study_03-07_004.pdf.

38. *Performance and Talent Management Trend Survey 2007*, available at http://www.successfactors.com/docs/performance-management-trends/2007/.

39. BusinessWeek Research Services for AARP, *Workers 50+: Business Executives' Attitudes Toward the Aging Workforce: Aware but Not Prepared?* (New York: BusinessWeek Services, 2006).

40. Robert Half International, *The Edge Report,* 2007, available at http://www.careerbuilder.com.

41. Deloitte, National Association of Manufacturers, and The Manufacturing Institute of America, *2005 Skills Gap Report: A Survey of the American Manufacturing Workforce,* http://www.nam.org/s_nam/bin.asp?CID=202426&DID=235731&DOC=FILE.PDF.

42. The exception was management and executive talent. Towers Perrin, *The Business Case for Workers Age 50+.*

43. Arlene Dohm and Lynn Shniper, "Occupational Employment Projections to 2016," *Monthly Labor Review,* November 2007, http://www.bls.gov/opub/mlr/2007/11/art5full.pdf.

44. The costs depend on how much of a search is required to fill the position, how much training and onboarding is necessary, etc. While it takes a fair amount of data to calculate a precise figure, once one has the data, doing so is straightforward. A Web site maintained by the University of

Wisconsin provides good software that will generate a precise estimate for any job: http://www.uwex.edu/ces/cced/economies/turn.cfm. An even more extensive set of software that includes estimates of the costs of lost knowledge is maintained by the Australian government: http://www.eowa.gov.au/Developing_a_Workplace_Program/Six_Steps_to_a_Workplace_Program/Step_2/_Costing_Turnover_Calculator/calc_home.htm.

45. *BusinessWeek* Research Services for AARP, *Workers 50+.* (Washington, DC: AARP).

46. Many studies make this point, but see, for example, Robert S. Huckman and Gary Pisano, "The Firm Specificity of Individual Performance: Evidence from Cardiac Surgery," *Management Science* 52, no. 4 (2006): 473–488, which finds that keeping the same team together in the same hospital is a key factor in surgical outcomes.

47. Bernard Hodes Group, *The 2006 Aging Nursing Workforce Survey,* http://www.hodes.com/industries/healthcare/resources/research/agingworkforce.asp.

48. Anne Fisher, "How to Battle the Coming Brain Drain," *Fortune,* March 21, 2005, 121–126.

49. Joe Mullich, "They Don't Retire Them, They Hire Them," *Workforce Management,* December 2003, 49–54.

50. According to Carnegie Mellon University's Electricity Industry Center.

51. Ibid.

52. Joan Williams and Cynthia Thomas Calvert, *Balanced Hours: Effective Part-time Policies for Washington Law Firms,* Final Report, 2nd ed. (San Francisco: Project for Attorney Retention, August 2001).

53. Pablo Martin de Holan, Nelson Phillips, and Thomas B. Lawrence, "Managing Organizational Forgetting," *MIT Sloan Management Review* (Winter 2004): 45–51.

54. Dorothy Leonard and Sylvia Sensiper, "The Role of Tacit Knowledge in Group Innovation," *California Management Review* 40, no. 3 (1998): 112–132.

55. Jennifer Reingold, "Brain Drain," *BusinessWeek,* September 20, 1999, 112.

56. Ibid.

57. Kate Blizard, Diversity Practice Lead, People and Performance, Business Financial Services, Westpac, "When Experience Matters" (presentation to The Conference Board, January 30, 2008).

58. These approaches are not a substitute for more systematic knowledge management practices, of course, as older workers can't stay engaged forever. These relationships buy time during which knowledge can be transferred.

59. AARP Best Employers Program Honoree, Argonne National Laboratory, 2007, http://www.aarp.org/money/careers/employerresourcecenter/bestemployers/winners/money/careers/employerresourcecenter/bestemployers/winners/argonne_national_laboratory.html.

60. Ken Dychtwald, Tamara J. Erickson, and Robert Morison, *Workforce Crisis* (Boston: Harvard Business School Press, 2006), 81.

61. Ibid., 92.

62. Fisher, "How to Battle the Coming Brain Drain."

63. Ibid.

Chapter 4

1. *Staying Ahead of the Curve: The AARP Work and Career Study,* national survey conducted for AARP by RoperASW, September 2002, http://assets.aarp.org/rgcenter/econ/d17773_multiwork_1.pdf.

2. C. S. Forte and C. L. Hansvick, "Applicant Age as a Subjective Employability Factor: A Study of Workers over and Under Age Fifty," *Journal of Employment Counseling* 36 (1999): 24–35. Older workers are biased toward older; younger workers biased toward younger.

3. A. L. Chasteen, N. Schwars, and D. C. Park, "The Activation of Aging Stereotypes in Younger and Older Adults," *Journal of Gerontology: Psychological Sciences* 57B (2002): 540–547.

4. L. M. Finkelstein and M. K. Burke, "Age Stereotyping at Work: The Role of Rater and Contextual Factors on Evaluations of Job Applicants," *Journal of General Psychology* 125, no. 4 (1998): 317–345.

5. Mary E. Kite et al., "Attitudes Toward Younger and Older Adults: An Updated Meta-Analytic Review," *Journal of Social Issues* 61, no. 2 (2005): 241–266.

6. See, e.g., W. C. K. Chiu et al., "Age Stereotypes and Discriminatory Attitudes Towards Older Workers: An East-West Comparison," *Human Relations* 54, no. 5 (2001): 629–661.

7. P. Taylor and A. Walker, "The Ageing Workforce: Employers' Attitudes Towards Older People," *Work, Employment and Society* 8 no. 4 (1994): 569–591.

8. For a discussion of the test, see Mary Lee Hummert et al., "Using the Implicit Association Test to Measure Age Differences in Implicit Social Cognitions," *Psychology and Aging* 17, no. 3 (2002): 482–495. For a summary of these results, see B. Levy and M. R. Banaji, "Implicit Ageism," in *Ageism: Stereotyping and Prejudice Against Older Persons*, ed. T. Nelson (Cambridge, MA: MIT Press, 2002), 49–75.

9. See, e.g., Hummert et al., "Using the Implicit Association Test."

10. *The Real Talent Debate: Will Aging Workers Deplete the Workforce?* Buck Consultants/Corporate Voices for Working Families/World at Work, 2006, http://www.cvworkingfamilies.org/downloads/TalentDebate.pdf?CFID=193 53334&CFTOKEN=68992183.

11. Alicia H. Munnell, Steven A. Sass, and Mauricio Soto, *Employer Attitudes Toward Older Workers: Survey Results, Work Opportunities for Older Americans,* Series 3 (Chestnut Hill, MA: Center for Retirement Research at Boston College, July 2006).

12. Marie Pitt-Catsouphes et al., *The National Study Report: Phase II of the National Study of Business Strategy and Workforce Development* (Chestnut Hill, MA: Center on Aging and Work at Boston College, 2007).

13. *The Real Talent Debate.*

14. Munnell, Sass, and Soto, *Employer Attitudes Toward Older Workers.* Employer attitudes outside the United States may be even more negative toward older workers. Survey data from Australia, for example, finds hiring managers rating older workers inferior to younger workers on twelve of twenty-eight work-related characteristics. See Eyal Gringart, Edward Helmes, and Craig Paul Speelman, "Exploring Attitudes Toward Older Workers Among Australian Employers: An Empirical Study," *Journal of Aging and Social Policy* 17, no. 3 (2005): 85–103.

15. About 3 percent of older men, for example, reported age discrimination in their current job, and of those who did, a disproportionate percentage ended up leaving the employer prematurely. See Richard W. Johnson and David Neumark, "Age Discrimination, Job Separations, and Employment Status of Older Workers: Evidence from Self-Reports," *Journal of Human Resources* 32, no. 4 (1997): 779–811.

16. *Staying Ahead of the Curve.*

17. It is true that a large proportion of charges are judged as being without merit, at least with respect to current legislative standards. But the charges that have been found by the EEOC to be without a legal basis have been falling, from 61 percent of the total in 1998 to 52 percent in 2008, and the dollar value of the settlements over the same period have roughly doubled. See http://www.eeoc.gov/stats.

18. David Neumark, "The Age Discrimination in Employment Act and the Challenge of Population Aging" (working paper 14317, National Bureau of Economic Research, Cambridge, MA, 2008, http://www.nber.org/papers/w14317).

19. Robert Hutchens, "Employer Willingness To Permit Phased Retirement: Why Are Some More Willing Than Others?" *Industrial & Labor Relations Review* 59, no. 4 (July 2006): 525–546.

20. Judith K. Hellerstein, David Neumark, and Kenneth R. Troske, "Wages, Productivity, and Worker Characteristics: Evidence from Plant-Level Production Functions and Wage Equations," *Journal of Labor Economics* 17, no. 3 (1999): 409–446.

21. R. A. Gordon and R. D. Arvey, "Age Bias in Laboratory and Field Settings: A Meta-analytic Investigation," *Journal of Applied Social Psychology* 34 (2004): 468–492.

22. See, e.g., Johnson and Neumark, *"Age Discrimination, Job Separations"*; and Scott J. Adams, "Passed Over for Promotion Because of Age: An Empirical Analysis of the Consequences," *Journal of Labor Research* 23, no. 3 (2002): 447–461. These studies also attempt to correct for self-serving biases—the fact that respondents who are passed over for promotion may be more inclined to see discrimination against people like them.

23. European Foundation for the Improvement of Living and Working Conditions, *Working Conditions of an Ageing Workforce* (Dublin, Ireland, 2008).

24. Dr. David DeLong, "The Paradox of the 'Working Retired': Identifying Barriers to Increased Labor Force Participation by Older Workers in the U.S." (Academy of Management, CMS Research Workshop, Managing the Aging Workforce: Leadership Towards a New Weltanschauung, August 11, 2006).

25. For surveys of these studies, see Maria Heidkamp and Carl E. Van Horn, *Older and Out of Work: Trends in Older Worker Displacement*, Issue Brief 16 (Sloan Center for Aging and Work at Boston College, September 2008); and Barry T. Hirsch, David A. MacPherson, and Melissa A. Hardy, "Occupational Age Structure and Access for Older Workers," *Industrial and Labor Relations Review* 53, no. 3 (2000): 401–418.

26. The main exception is for "high policy-making employees" with a defined benefit pension of $44,000 per year, having been in that position for the prior two years. This exemption seems to be used mainly by professional services firms whose chairs or managing partners often have mandatory retirement at sixty-five, or in the accounting world more typically at age sixty.

27. Lynn Selhat, interview with author, Philadelphia, 2007.

28. For surveys of these studies, see Heidkamp and Van Horn, *Older and Out of Work*; and Hirsch, MacPherson, and Hardy, "Occupational Age Structure and Access."

29. Lynne Bennington, "Age Discrimination: Converging Evidence from Four Australian Studies," *Employee Responsibilities and Rights Journal* 13, no. 3 (2001): 125–134.

30. For a review of the research on this topic, see David Neumark, "Age Discrimination Legislation in the United States" (working paper W8152, National Bureau of Economic Research, Cambridge, MA, 2001).

31. Joanna Lahey, "Age, Women, and Hiring: An Experimental Study," *Journal of Human Resources* 43 (2008): 30–56.

32. Marc Bendick Jr., Lauren E. Brown, and Kennington Wall, "No Foot in the Door: An Experimental Study of Employment Discrimination Against Older Workers," *Journal of Aging and Social Policy* 10, no. 4 (1999): 5–24.

33. Domestic & General is a 2008 AARP International Innovative Employer Award recipient where this practice is described.

34. Frederick Morgeson et al., "Review of Research on Age Discrimination in the Employment Interview," *Journal of Business and Psychology* 22, no. 3 (2008): 223–232.

35. Peter Cappelli, "Why Is It So Hard to Find Information Technology Workers?" *Organizational Dynamics* 30, no. 2 (2001): 87–99.

36. Ibid.

37. Levy and Banaji, "Implicit Ageism."

38. Becca R. Levy, Martin D. Slade, Suzanne R. Kunkel, and Stanislav V. Kasl, "Longevity Increased by Positive Self-Perceptions of Aging," *Journal of Personality & Social Psychology* 83, no. 2 (August 2002): 261–270.

Chapter 5

1. *The Real Talent Debate: Will Aging Workers Deplete the Workforce?* Buck Consultants/Corporate Voices for Working Families/World at Work, 2006, http://www.cvworkingfamilies.org/downloads/TalentDebate.pdf?CFID=193 53334&CFTOKEN=68992183; and Dan Kadlec, "The Generation Gap at Work," CNNMoney.com, http://money.cnn.com/2007/11/01/pf/100710960. moneymag/.

2. The study is reported in Patricia Kitchen, "Aging Boomer Workers Confront Reality of Younger Bosses," *Newsday*, January 22, 2005.

3. BusinessWeek Research Services for AARP, *Workers 50+: Business Executives' Attitudes Toward the Aging Workforce: Aware but Not Prepared?* (New York: BusinessWeek Services, 2006); and W. J. Smith and K. V. Harrington, "Younger Supervisor-Older Subordinate Dyads: A Relationship of Cooperation or Resistance?" *Psychological Reports* 74, no. 3 (1994): 803–812.

4. *Older Employees in the Workforce—A Companion Brief to: Generation and Gender in the Workplace* (New York: Families and Work Institute, 2002), http://familiesandwork.org/site/research/reports/olderworkers.pdf.

5. Anne S. Tsui and Charles A. O'Reilly III, "Beyond Simple Demographic Effects: The Importance of Relational Demography in Superior-Subordinate Dyads," *Academy of Management Journal* 32, no. 2 (1989): 402–423.

6. G. R. Ferrris et al., "The Age Context of Performance Evaluation Decisions," *Psychology and Aging* 6 (1991): 616–626.

7. Mary E. Kite et al., "Attitudes Toward Younger and Older Adults: An Updated Meta-Analytic Review," *Journal of Social Issues* 61, no. 2 (2005): 241–266.

8. Cheri Ostroff and Leanne E. Atwater, "Does Whom You Work With Matter? Effects of Referent Group Gender and Age Composition on Managers' Compensation," *Journal of Applied Psychology* 88, no. 4 (2003): 725–740.

9. Samuel B. Bacharach, Peter Bamberger, and Bryan Mundell, "Status Inconsistency in Organizations: From Social Hierarchy to Stress," *Journal of Organizational Behavior* 14, no. 1 (1993): 21–36.

10. See, for example, Gerald R. Ferris et al., "The Influence of Subordinate Age on Performance Ratings and Causal Attributions," *Personnel Psychology* 38, no. 3 (1985): 545–557.

11. Esther J. Dedrick and Gregory H. Dobbins, "The Influence of Subordinate Age on Managerial Actions: An Attributional Analysis," *Journal of Organizational Behavior* 12, no. 5 (1991): 367–377.

12. Robert C. Liden, Dean Stilwell, and Gerald R. Ferris, "The Effects of Supervisor and Subordinate Age on Objective Performance and Subjective Performance Ratings," *Human Relations* 49, no. 3 (1996): 327.

13. A. S. Tsui, K. R. Xin, and T. D. Egan, "Relational Demography: The Missing Link in Vertical Dyad Linkage," in *Diversity in Work Teams*, eds. S. E. Jackson and M. N. Ruderman (Washington, DC: American Psychological Association, 1995), 97–129.

14. Mary Hair Collins, Joseph F. Hair Jr., and Tonette S. Rocco, "The Older-Worker-Younger-Supervisor Dyad: A Test of the Reverse Pygmalion Effect," *Human Resource Development Quarterly* 20, no. 1 (Spring 2009): 21–41.

15. Gary Charness and Marie-Claire Villeval, "Cooperation and Competition in Intergenerational Experiments in the Field and the Laboratory," *American Economic Review* 99, no. 3 (2009): 956–978.

16. See, e.g., Ruth Kanfer and Phillip L. Ackerman, "Aging, Adult Development, and Work Motivation," *Academy of Management Review* 29, no. 3 (2004): 440–458.

17. L. L. Carstensen, "A Life-Span Approach to Social Motivation," in *Motivation and Self-Regulation Across the Life Span*, eds. J. Heckhausen and C. S. Dweck (New York: Cambridge University Press, 1998), 341–364.

18. J. D. McAdams, "Generativity in Midlife," in *Handbook of Midlife Development,* ed. M. E. Lachman (New York: John Wiley & Sons, 2001), 395–443.

19. See, e.g., Jutta Heckhausen and Richard Schulz, "A Life Span Model of Successful Aging," *American Psychologist* 51, no. 7 (1996): 702–714.

20. D. C. Treadway et al., "The Role of Age in the Perceptions of Politics-Job Performance Relationship: A Three-Study Constructive Replication," *Journal of Applied Psychology* 90 (2005): 872–881.

21. M. R. Barrick, and M. K. Mount, "The Big Five Personality Dimensions and Job Performance: A Meta-Analysis," *Personnel Psychology* 44, (1991): 1–26.

22. B. W. Roberts, K. E. Walton, and W. Viechtbauer, "Patterns of Mean-Level Change in Personality Traits Across the Life Course: A Meta-analysis of Longitudinal Studies," *Psychological Bulletin* 132 (2006): 1–25.

23. Mathias Allemand, Daniel Zimprich, and A. A. Jolijn Hendriks, "Age Differences in Five Personality Domains Across the Life Span," *Developmental Psychology* 44, no. 3 (2008): 758–770.

24. *The Business Case for Workers Age 50+: Planning for Tomorrow's Talent Needs in Today's Competitive Environment,* report for AARP prepared by Towers Perrin, December 2005, http://assets.aarp.org/rgcenter/econ/workers_fifty_plus_1.pdf.

25. Ellen Galinsky, "The Changing Landscape of Work," *Generations* 31, no. 1 (2007): 16–22.

26. Lacy G. Urbantke, "In Young Company: Supervisor Strategies for Managing Conflict with Older Subordinates" (PhD diss., Baylor University, 2006), http://hdl.handle.net/2104/4201.

27. Elissa Perry, Carol J. Kulick, and Jing Zhou, "A Closer Look at the Effects of Supervisor-Subordinate Age Differences," *Journal of Organizational Behavior* 20 (1999): 341–357.

28. Jerry David, e-mail correspondence with authors, 2007.

29. Jon R. Katzenbach and Jason A. Santamaria, "Firing Up the Front Line," *Harvard Business Review,* May–June 1999, 107–117.

30. Harvey Sterns, interview by author, October 15, 2009.

Chapter 6

1. European Foundation for the Improvement of Living and Working Conditions, *Working Conditions of an Ageing Workforce* (Dublin, EuroFound, May 2008).

2. Dr. David DeLong, "The Paradox of the 'Working Retired': Identifying Barriers to Increased Labor Force Participation by Older Workers in the U.S."

(Academy of Management, CMS Research Workshop, Managing the Aging Workforce: Leadership Towards a New Weltanschauung, August 11, 2006).

3. RetirementJobs.com, "Flexibility Ranks First, Entrepreneurship Last, When Baby Boomers and Active Retirees Seek Retirement Jobs, According to New Survey from RetirementJobs.com," news release, June 21, 2006, http://www.retirementjobs.com/aboutus/press/06_21_2006.html.

4. Marcie Pitt-Catsouphes and Michael A. Smyer, "Aging and the Meaning of Work," http://agingandwork.bc.edu/template_meaning_of_work.

5. AARP, "What Older Workers Want," http://www.aarp.org/money/careers/employerresourcecenter/trends/a2004-04-20-olderworkers.html.

6. Interview with author.

7. See Richard W. Johnson, Janette Kawachi, and Eric K. Lewis, *Older Workers on the Move: Recareering in Later Life* (Washington, DC: AARP Public Policy Institute, 2009). The possibility that they are rationalizing their decisions no doubt explains some of the increased satisfaction.

8. A complete list of attributes would also include working in jobs with a greater variety of tasks, getting feedback on one's performance, and working on tasks big enough to be thought of as a meaningful unit of output (e.g., assembling an engine rather than simply placing parts on the engine). This famous framework in the psychology of work is known as job design and is useful for workers of any age (see J. R. Hackman and G. R. Oldham, *Work Redesign* (Reading, MA: Addison-Wesley, 1980).

9. A very brief description of the program is provided at http://www.gsk.com/responsibility/cr-review-2007/downloads/employment.pdf.

10. 13 AARP, "Flexible Work Arrangements Attract Older Workers," http://www.aarp.org/money/careers/employerresourcecenter/retention/a2004-12-17-flexiblework.html.

11. Anne Fisher, "How to Battle the Coming Brain Drain," *Fortune*, March 21, 2005, 121–127.

12. Bob Moos, "Go for The Golden: More Companies Prize Older Workers for Lifetime of Know-How," *Dallas Morning News*, October 23, 2005, http://www.zey.com/ceilidh/44c5ab05Xzu-5851-828-00.htm.

13. Mary Young, Diane Piktialis, and Anna Rappaport, *Gray Skies, Silver Linings*, Research Report R-1409-07-RR (New York: Conference Board, 2007).

14. K. A. Phillippe and M. J. Valiga, *Faces of the Future: Summary Findings* (Washington, DC: ACT and American Association of Community Colleges, 2000).

15. AARP, "Adecco, Winning Strategies 2006," http://www.aarp.org/money/careers/employerresourcecenter/bestemployers/winners/adecco.html.

16. AARP, "Lee Memorial Health System, Winning Strategies 2006," http://www.aarp.org/money/careers/employerresourcecenter/bestemployers/ winners/lee_memorial.html.

17. Peter Cappelli, "Why Do Employers Pay for College?" *Journal of Econometrics* 121, no. 1–2 (2004): 213–241.

18. AARP, "Bon Secours Richmond Health System, Winning Strategies 2006," http//www.aarp.org/money/careers/employerresourcecenter/ bestemployers/winners/bon_secours_richmond.html.

19. Anna Rappaport and Matt Stevenson, *Staying Ahead of the Curve 2004: Employer Best Practices for Mature Workers*, D18178 (Washington, DC: AARP, September 2004), 25–59.

20. "The Aging Workforce," *Hospitals & Health Networks* 82, no. 1 (2008), http://www.hhnmag.com/hhnmag_app/jsp/hhnonline.jsp.

21. Gace A. Odums, "A New Year's Resolution: Optimize Older Workers," *T+D*, January 2006, 34–36.

22. Leslie Stevens-Huffman, "Turning to Niche Staffing Firms to Fill In Specialized Hiring Needs," *Workforce Management*, March 13, 2006, 50–51, http://www.workforce.com/archive.

23. Job seekers can visit the National Employer Team Web site to learn more about the specific companies and link directly to their jobs pages; see http://www.aarp.org/money/work/articles/national_employer_team.html. Other sites that help older workers find jobs include ExperienceWorks.org, RetirementJobs.com, Seniors4Hire.org, RetireeWorkForce.com, WorkForce50. com, RetiredBrains.com, YourEncore.com, and MatureServices.org.

24. Kate Blizard, Diversity Practice Lead, People and Performance, Business Financial Services, Westpac, "When Experience Matters" (presentation to The Conference Board, January 30, 2008).

25. Joyce Russell, interview with Lynn Selhat, 2007.

26. Bernadette Kenney, interview with Lynn Selhat, 2007.

27. Gerri Willis and Lauren Young, "Retire Happy," *Smart Money*, March 8, 2010, http://www.smartmoney.com/personal-finance/retirement/retire-happy-14118/.

28. Marilyn Elias, "Retirees Back at Work, with Flexibility: Many Also Spend Fewer Hours on the Job," *USA Today*, June 9, 2005, http://www. agewave.com/media_files/usaretiree.html.

29. Jennifer Reingold, "Brain Drain," *BusinessWeek*, September 20, 1999, 112.

30. Fisher, "How to Battle the Coming Brain Drain."

31. Ken, Dychtwald, Tamara J. Erickson, and Robert Morison, *Workforce Crisis* (Boston: Harvard Business School Press, 2006), 49–50.

32. AARP, "Bon Secours Richmond Health System."

33. A good overview of these arrangements is in William J. Rothwell et al., *Working Longer: New Strategies for Managing, Training, and Retaining Older Workers* (New York: AMACOM, 2008). Chapter 2 describes accommodations for age-related impairments like hearing and vision loss, while chapter 5 outlines unique approaches for training older workers (e.g., slower pace, more practice, more support).

Chapter 7

1. Bill Novelli with Boe Workman, *Fifty Plus: Give Meaning and Purpose to the Best Time of Your Life* (New York: Macmillan, 2007).

2. Steve Gillon, *Boomer Nation: The Largest and Richest Generation Ever, and How It Changed America*. (New York: Free Press, 2004).

3. Novelli, *Fifty Plus*, 146.

4. Nicholas J. Thompson and Keith E. Thompson, "Can Marketing Practice Keep Up with Europe's Ageing Population?" *European Journal of Marketing* 43, no. 11–12 (2009): 1281.

5. Focalyst Boomer Segmentation Study conducted for AARP, 2008.

6. Lynn Sudbury and Peter Simcock, "A Multivariate Segmentation Model of Senior Consumers," *Journal of Consumer Marketing* 26, no. 4 (2009): 251.

Index

About the Authors

Peter Cappelli is the George W. Taylor Professor of Management at The Wharton School and Director of Wharton's Center for Human Resources. He is also a Research Associate at the National Bureau of Economic Research in Cambridge, MA. He previously served as Senior Advisor to the Kingdom of Bahrain for Employment Policy, and since 2007 has been a Distinguished Scholar of Singapore's Ministry of Manpower. He has degrees in industrial relations from Cornell University and in labor economics from Oxford University, where he was a Fulbright Scholar. He has been a Guest Scholar at the Brookings Institution, a German Marshall Fund Fellow, and a faculty member at MIT, the University of Illinois, and the University of California, Berkeley.

Professor Cappelli was recently named by Vault.com as one the twenty-five most important people working in the area of human capital, one of the top 100 people in the field of recruiting and staffing by Recruit.com, and was elected a fellow of the National Academy of Human Resources. He received the 2009 PRO award from the International Association of Corporate and Professional Recruiters for contributions to human resources. He currently serves on commissions for The Business Roundtable, the World Economic Forum, and the U.S. Department of Labor.

Professor Cappelli's recent research examines changes in employment relations in the United States and their implications. He is the author of many books, including *The New Deal at Work* (Harvard Business School Press, 1999) and *Talent on Demand* (Harvard Business Press, 2008) (named a "best business book" for 2008 by

Booz-Allen), and the coauthor of *The India Way* (Harvard Business Review Press, 2010).

Bill Novelli is a Distinguished Professor in the McDonough School of Business at Georgetown University. He teaches in the MBA program and is working to establish an Initiative on Social Enterprise. For nearly a decade, he was CEO of AARP, a membership organization of 40 million people age fifty and older. During his tenure, the organization achieved major policy, growth, and international successes.

Bill earlier was president of the Campaign for Tobacco-Free Kids and now serves as chairman of its board. He was also executive vice president of CARE and oversaw operations both in the United States and abroad. Previously, he cofounded Porter Novelli, now one of the largest PR agencies in the world and part of the Omnicom Group, an international marketing communications company. He retired from Porter Novelli to pursue a second career in public service. He is a recognized leader in social marketing and social change in the United States and internationally.

Bill began his career at Unilever, moved to a New York ad agency, and then to Washington to help market the Peace Corps. His book, *Fifty Plus: Give Meaning and Purpose to the Best Time of Your Life,* was updated in 2008. He holds a BA from the University of Pennsylvania and an MA from Penn's Annenberg School for Communication, and pursued doctoral studies at New York University. Bill serves on a number of boards and committees. He lives in Bethesda, MD with his wife, Fran. They have three adult children and seven grandchildren.